Michael H. Macnamara

The Irish Ninth in Bivouac and Battle

Or Virginia and Maryland Campaigns

Michael H. Macnamara

The Irish Ninth in Bivouac and Battle
Or Virginia and Maryland Campaigns

ISBN/EAN: 9783744740357

Printed in Europe, USA, Canada, Australia, Japan

Cover: Foto ©ninafisch / pixelio.de

More available books at **www.hansebooks.com**

THE IRISH NINTH

IN BIVOUAC AND BATTLE;

OR,

VIRGINIA AND MARYLAND CAMPAIGNS.

BY

M. H. MACNAMARA,

LATE CAPTAIN NINTH MASS. VOLS.

> "Patriots have toiled, and in their country's cause
> Bled nobly; and their deeds, as they deserve,
> Receive proud recompense. We give in charge
> Their names to the sweet lyre. The historic muse,
> Proud of the treasure, marches with it down
> To latest times."

> "He sunk to repose where the red heaths are blended;
> One dream of his childhood his fancy passed o'er;
> But his battles are fought, and his march it is ended;
> The sound of the bugle shall wake him no more."

BOSTON:
LEE AND SHEPARD.
1867.

TO

MADAM HARRISON GRAY OTIS,

The Patroness of the Ninth Regiment,

AND THE LADY WHOSE PRACTICAL INTEREST IN THE WELFARE
OF THE FEDERAL SOLDIERS

PLACES HER FIRST AMONG THE PATRIOTIC WOMEN OF NEW ENGLAND,

THIS BOOK IS RESPECTFULLY DEDICATED,

BY THE AUTHOR.

BOSTON, March 11, 1867.

MESSRS. LEE & SHEPARD.

GENTLEMEN: By your kindness I have been shown the proof sheets of Captain Macnamara's book, entitled "THE IRISH NINTH IN BIVOUAC AND BATTLE." You have also done me the honor to request my opinion of its merits.

On account of my own intimate relation to the subject matter of the book, I feel disinclined to say so much in its praise as, under other circumstances, I would be glad to say. But perhaps this relation should not, nor does it, deter me from expressing my approbation of its general historic accuracy.

Respectfully,
Your obedient servant,
P. R. GUINEY,
Late Col. Ninth Mass. and Brevet Brig.-Gen. Vols.

PREFACE.

PROMPTED by a desire to show the world how well the Irishmen, exiled from their native land by the ruthless system of English law practised in Ireland, can serve their adopted country in the day of her trial, and being solicitous that the record of their services should survive the few who remain of "the Irish Ninth," and go down to the posterity of all who fought in its ranks, the author presents this volume to the public.

The incidents and events which constitute the basis, and perhaps the value, of the following pages, were noted in a diary as they occurred, amid the varied scenes through which we passed during three years of active military service. In addition to these personal facilities, we have availed ourselves of official data, obligingly placed at our disposal, in order to make the regimental roster unquestionably accurate.

The author has also a subordinate purpose in presenting so much of a descriptive character. He hopes in this manner to give the public some idea of the way in which Irish soldiers turn the "horrors of war" into the most enjoyable of festivities, and to recall to the minds of his comrades some of the many happy scenes which he shared with them under the canvas in the far-off and sunny South.

CONTENTS.

CHAPTER I.
PAGE

The Response to the President's Call. — Colonel Cass tenders his Services to the State. — His Offer accepted. — The Raising of the Regiment. — Recruits and Recruiting. — Drilling Difficulties. — Election of Officers. — Original Muster Roll. — Removal from Boston to Long Island. 13

CHAPTER II

Long Island, Description of. — Arranging our Camp. — Rapid Acquisition of Military Discipline. — A Sunday at Long Island. — Reflections. 23

CHAPTER III.

Social Parties. — The valiant Sentinel. — Plain, plain Tom. . 31

CHAPTER IV.

Leaving Long Island. — A false Alarm. — Arrival at Washington. — Emmart's Farm. — The Captain and his Dog; or, Discipline versus Sagacity. 35

CHAPTER V.

Summary Treatment of Poachers. — An Unfortunate Rencontre. — Our Valiant Pickets, Pedlers, and Hawkers. — Rumors of a Move. — Bull Run. — Our Night March, and speedy Return to Camp. 42

CHAPTER VI.

Our retreating Forces. — Scenes on the Way. — We march for Arlington. — Our gratifying Reception. 49

CHAPTER VII.

Arlington. — General Lee's House. — A Negress. — How Lee kept a dying Wish. — A good Breakfast. — Negroes and Negro Minstrels. — We resume our March. 55

CHAPTER VIII.

We occupy the Heights. — Fort Cass. — The Cow Bell. — Pleasant Society. — "Balls Hamilton." — We are presented with Colors. — McClellan organizes the Army. — Grand Review. . 61

CHAPTER IX.

We leave Arlington. — Arrive at Miner's Hill. — Painful Scene. — Many killed and wounded. — Colonel Cass' Opinion. — How we kept Christmas. — Lieutenant-Colonel Peard dies. — Fairfax. — A March in the Rain. — Alexandria. 71

CHAPTER X

Our Bonnie Green Flag. — We reach Hampton, Va. — A Reconnoissance. — We march for Yorktown. — Our Men dig In-

trenchments. — The Evacuation of Yorktown. — We start for
"West Point." — Columbia Landing. — White House. —
Gaines' Mills and Hanover Court House. — An Engagement.
— A Noble Deed. 79

CHAPTER XI.

Our Captain and the General. — Mechanicsville. — Battle of
Gaines' Mills. — Battle of the Chickahominy — Our Position
after the Battle. — Night Scenes. 93

CHAPTER XII.

Malvern Hill. — The Battle. — Gallant Charges. — Death of
Colonel Cass. — Is succeeded by Colonel Guiney — Harrison's
Landing. — A Scare. — Straps and no Straps. — A Night's
Rest disturbed. 105

CHAPTER XIII.

We leave Harrison's Landing. — Visit Miner's Hill. — Sad Recollections. — McClellan again resumes Command. — Invasion of
Maryland. — Battle of Antietam. — Retreat of Lee. . . . 114

CHAPTER XIV.

Scenes at Antietam and South Mountain. — The doomed Legion.
— Insults offered to Union Soldiers. — Hospital Scenes. —
Yankee Smartness. — Be careful of your Stars. — It is finished. — A miscreant Regiment. — Goteler's Mills. — Picket
Duty. — End of first Maryland Campaign. 119

CHAPTER XV.

Crossing the Potomac under Difficulties. — Shepherdstown. —
Rebel Chaff. — That was all it was fit for. — A neat Thing in

Shawls. — We find the Enemy. — Return to Camp. — Sharpsburg. 128

CHAPTER XVI.

A social Evening. — Presence of Mind. — A startling Narrative. — A Cure for Bores. — How it was effected. 136

CHAPTER XVII.

How the Soldier leaves an old Camp. — Maryland Heights. — A Night March. — Harper's Ferry. — Surrounding Prospect. — John Brown's House. — Snicker's Gap. — We march to Warrenton. — McClellan superseded. — Stoneman's Station. 147

CHAPTER XVIII.

The Siege of Fredericksburg. — The gallant Irish Brigade. — First Day. — The Second Day. — In Position. — General Humphrey. — Expectation. — We sleep on the Field. . . . 156

CHAPTER XIX.

The Continuation of the Siege. — Very near. — It takes an Irishman to crack a Joke. — Our hopeless Position. — We evacuate the Heights. — The sacked City. — How to be jolly under any Circumstances. —A Presentation. — We return to Falmouth. 162

CHAPTER XX.

Winter Quarters. — Those Pies. — Punch. — The Child of the Forest. — A Reconnoissance to Barnett's Ford. — Sharp Marching. — Horse Racing. — How we spent St. Patrick's Day. — Fatal Accident. 171

CHAPTER XXI.

The Regiment is presented with a new Flag. — We leave Falmouth. — Kelley's Ford. — Ellis' Ford. — The Battle of Chancellorsville. — The Plank Road. — A wrong Turn. — How the Doctors were routed. — Ellis' Ford. — Sketch of Mr. Ellis. — To Brandy Station. — Encounter with the Enemy. — Tough Marching. — Bad Luck to this Marching. 182

CHAPTER XXII.

General Meade assumes Command. — Gettysburg. — Following the Enemy. — We reënter Virginia. — The Professor's Excuse for Lagging. — He could not rob the Dead. 194

CHAPTER XXIII.

Incidents of a March. — A dirty Musket. — The Colonel and the Corporal. — An ungrateful Man. — Retaliation. — More of the Professor. — How he got his Larnin. 201

CHAPTER XXIV.

Rectorstown. — How to estimate Compliments. — Wapping Heights. — Warrenton. — The Landlord played out. — Beverley Ford. — Our Camp. — Arrival of Conscripts. — We march for Culpepper. 209

CHAPTER XXV.

Culpepper. — Insinuating Females. — Picket Duty. — Drummed Out. — Speculations. — Guerrillas. — "De ole Man's a grazing eber since." — A "What is it?" — A Negro Gymnast. — A crazy Professor. — Uncle Jolly and his good kind Sisters . . 215

CHAPTER XXVI.

Rainy Weather. — Damp Meditations. — The Rapidan before. — The Rappahannock behind. — Counter Strategy. — Bull Run. — The old Battle-ground. — The Death of Kearney. — Graves of the gallant Dead. — The dead Sentinel. — Heroic Mementos. — March to Gainesville. — Army Wagons rolling over the Dead. 226

CHAPTER XXVII.

A Rebel Camp. — Rebel Sufferings and Rebel Sympathizers. — Condition of Rebel Camps. — Of Union Camps. — Preserve us from the Attributes of Southern Chivalry. — New Baltimore. — Auburn. — Three-mile Station. — Rappahannock Station. — Storming the Enemy's Works. — Brandy Station. — General Meade and his Movements. — The Ninth in the Position of Honor and Danger. — The Invitation to Death. — Description of Mine Run. — Winter Quarters. — Bealton. . 233

CHAPTER XXVIII.

Bealton Station. — Winter Duties. — Mosby's Guerrillas. — Black Horse Cavalry. — Cutting Railroads. — Vigilance and Valor. — A March. — The coming Wilderness. — The Battle of the Wilderness. — Irish Heroism. — Spottsylvania. — Bethesda Church. — Shady Oak. — Cold Harbor. — The Dead. — Home and Muster-out. 242

APPENDIX.

ROSTER OF OFFICERS. 247
    "   ENLISTED MEN. 258

THE IRISH NINTH

IN

BIVOUAC AND BATTLE.

CHAPTER I.

The Response to the President's Call. — Colonel Cass tenders his Services to the State. — His Offer accepted. — The Raising of the Regiment. — Recruits and Recruiting. — Drilling Difficulties. — Election of Officers. — Original Muster Roll. — Removal from Boston to Long Island.

THE wires that flashed the news of the fall of Fort Sumter touched with their electricity, not only the brain, but the great heart of the nation, stimulating the patriotism of a peaceful people, and awakening an energy which for a time submerged the business transactions of quiet communities in the preparations for the great and eventful struggle which was to decide the supremacy of the Federal Government and the stability of the American Constitution.

The warlike proclivities of the American people became immediately manifest. The desecration of the American flag not only fired with indignation the native, but awakened the patriotism of the foreign element, so that, in a few short hours, there were congregated on "Change" and in the public places, groups and bodies of indignant citizens, who loudly vowed the vengeance since inflicted upon the treacherous states which so grossly insulted the sacred flag, beneath whose folds so much honor had been achieved, and under the light of whose stars the American nation marched to prosperity and success.

Immediately after the fall of Fort Sumter the President of the United States issued a call for seventy-five thousand men, which were rapidly supplied by the militia of the country, and sent into the field for three months. Shortly after this the President issued a second call for three hundred thousand volunteers, and preparations upon a grand and extensive scale were immediately made for the enlistment, quartering, and equipment of the quota of the several states.

The enthusiasm of the people of Massachusetts was of the first order. Flags were flung to the breeze from public buildings and private dwellings in every part of the capital of Massachusetts; recruiting offices were opened, and large handbills posted in every place of prominence in Boston. The excitement and enthusiasm throughout the city were intense, and enlistments rapidly progressed. Such was the state of affairs when, early in the month of April, CAPTAIN CASS, then commanding the Columbian Asscciation, proposed to the Governor of Massachusetts to raise an Irish regiment for three years, under the call of the President of the United States, or for a longer period if they were required.

The proposition of Captain Cass was considered by the Governor of Massachusetts, and in a short time cordially accepted; and, furnished with the documents authorizing the organization, Captain Cass made immediate preparations for the formation of a regiment, opened recruiting offices under the control of competent gentlemen, and in a short time the enlistments were so rapid as to give every augury of success. Agents were despatched to every part of Massachusetts, and able speakers created an influence in favor of the great work that soon established a military ardor which placed the success of the regiment beyond question. The writer can recall many instances where men, stalwart and robust young Irishmen, travelled many miles on foot for the purpose of enlisting in "Captain Cass' Irish Regiment;" men who, having read of the glory of "*The Old Brigade,*" felt tingling in their veins the martial ardor that actuated the Irish exiles in France, when, under the *fleur de lys*, they won so much glory, and shed so much blood.

It is not wonderful that with material like this the "Irish Ninth" would win imperishable renown. The writer has often noticed a distinguishing characteristic of the Irish recruit in painful contrast with the sordid exactions of some native soldiers. An Irish recruit would enter an office, and declare his intention of enlisting; you would explain to him his obligations; he would listen as though he had not the slightest interest in your remarks; and when you had concluded, he would ask (if he could write), "Give me the pen!" In a moment his name would be down, while, on the other hand, a native would argue for an hour, discuss the terms, time of enlistment, and finally wind up the long colloquy by naively asking, what chance there was for a commission, for which he would be as well fitted as "*Balls Hamilton*," an "intelligent contraband," who once figured in a minor capacity with the regiment in Western Virginia, and who will enact a conspicuous part in another chapter of our work.

Many of our best soldiers were men of family and position, comfortably situated, who entered the service from feelings of pure patriotism and warm affection for a government under which they had long lived and their children had been born. To them the stars and stripes was a beautiful emblem; and if they could not love it as dearly as their own native green, they could fight for it as bravely, and shed their blood for it as freely, as any "to the manor born."

The process of induction at that time was exceedingly rapid; a man was enlisted, carried before the surgeon, pronounced fit or unfit for military service; if accepted, sent to a boarding-house, — for the state had no barracks, — and the next day initiated into the mysteries of the first position of a soldier, which initiation sometimes made the joints crack and provoked the innocent exclamation, "Ah! but it's the divil's own way to stand!" and when told to be silent, would obey you by saying, "Sure I'm not spaking, sur," which, when he had concluded, would be undoubtedly true.

When the recruit was perfect in the preliminary, he would be tried in the serious and complex "right face." This movement, in the outset, gave rise to a medley of queer turns and twists. One would face by the left, and look with an expression of gratified pride upon his face into the eyes of his neighbor, whose position was correct, feeling perfectly satisfied that *he* was right and his comrade wrong. When corrected, his face would assume a very sheepish expression, and with a droll twinkle in his eye, he would say, "Was it by the right ye mane? O, we'll do it over agin." This time you would command "left face," and, sure enough, the gallant fellow would face by the right. The countenance of the Irish soldier bears a very solemn expression while on drill — more solemn than that of the Jew who declares himself swindled in the midst of his richest bargain. The Irish recruit is, notwithstanding, a very rapid learner, and more readily grasps the principles of a movement than the soldiers of other nations.

Recruiting in Boston at that time was not the dreary routine it afterwards became; the excitement was very great, and enlistments rapid; yet the recruiting officer had many serious obstacles to contend with. Not having a proper place of security for the recruits, many of them, growing restless, would become invisible, — some for a time, and some forever, — leaving you the genial employment of liquidating sundry board bills, and mentally reckoning the brokerage value of sundry little loans, which, when your martial heart overflowed with generosity, you had kindly transferred from your own pocket to that of the faithless invisible. However, these were minor trials, and we all got used to them, and in a short time became, in our own conceit, "uncommonly sharp on the recruit."

In the short period of three weeks the Ninth Regiment, then unnumbered and without a name, was called together at the rooms of the Columbian Association, which had been kindly tendered by that patriotic body for the purpose, and there it was equalized and formed into companies, and arrangements made for the election of officers, which took place at the rooms of the Columbian Association and at the temporary barracks in Lindall Street. The election concluded, the officers passed the ordeal of examination — and ordeal it was, in more senses than one — at the State House, and in a short time received the state commissions from His Excellency, Governor John A. Andrew. As these commissions were received by the original founders of the regiment, we feel it our duty to append the following roster of names: —

THOMAS CASS,	Colonel.
C. G. ROWELL,	Lieutenant-Colonel.
ROBERT PEARD,	Major.
PETER PINEO,	Surgeon.
PATRICK A. O'CONNELL,	Assistant Surgeon.
THOMAS SCULLY,	Chaplain.
GEO. W. PERKINS,	Adjutant.
MICHAEL SCANLAN,	Quartermaster.
JAMES E. GALLAGHER,	Captain, Company A.
CHRISTOPHER PLUNKETT,	" " B.
WILLIAM MADIGAN,	" " C.
JAMES J. PENDERGAST,	" " D.
M. H. MACNAMARA,	" " E.
EDWARD FITZGERALD,	" " F.
JOHN CAREY,	" " G.
JEREMIAH O'NIELL,	" " H.
BERNARD S. TREANOR,	" " I.
GEO. W. DUTTON,	" " K.

Francis O'Dowd,	1st Lieutenant,	Company	A.
Patrick T. Hanley,	" "	"	B.
John W. Mahan,	" "	"	C.
Archibald Simpson,	" "	"	D.
James E. McCafferty, Jr.	" "	"	E.
Timothy O'Leary,	" "	"	F.
John M. Tobin,	" "	"	G.
Thomas K. Roach,	" "	"	H.
P. R. Guiney,	" "	"	I.
James E. McGunnigle,	" "	"	K.
M. F. O'Hara,	2d Lieutenant,	Company	A.
John H. Walsh,	" "	"	B.
Edward McSweeney,	" "	"	C.
J. H. Rafferty,	" "	"	D.
J. W. Macnamara,	" "	"	E.
Philip Redmond,	" "	"	F.
Timothy Burke,	" "	"	H.
Richard P. Nugent,	" "	"	I.
Joseph Ford,	" "	"	K.

By the addition of four fine companies from Milford, Stoughton, Marlboro', and Salem, under the respective commands of Captains Peard (afterwards major), Carey, Dutton, and Fitzgerald, valuable and gallant officers, the two former of whom have since offered up their lives in defence of the flag of their adopted country, the minimum number of the regiment was reached, and thus the organization of the Ninth

Massachusetts Volunteers was completed, and by order of the Governor, and with the consent of Mayor Wightman, of Boston, the regiment was marched to Faneuil Hall, then used as barracks, where they were supplied with quarters and rations until their removal to Long Island, in Boston Harbor, which took place in May, 1861.

CHAPTER II.

Long Island, Description of. — Arranging our Camp. — Rapid Acquisition of Military Discipline. — A Sunday at Long Island. — Reflections.

AMONG the many pleasing memories associated with the formation of the Ninth Regiment, there are none so delightful as those connected with its sojourn on Long Island.

The local reader is well acquainted with the geographical position of that pleasant and healthy military rendezvous; but a few words for the benefit of those unacquainted with that lovely island may not be amiss. It is situated in Boston harbor, and distant about four miles from Boston proper, and from South and East Boston distant about one mile and a half; elongated in form, about a mile from point to point. A large public house stands upon the island, which has always been a favorite summer resort. The island, as I remember, was, upon the south side, thickly studded with trees; a beautiful verdure clothed the miniature valleys, and of a summer morning, when the sea was calm and the red glory of a summer sunrise looked down upon the dotted camp ground, the scene was inexpressibly beautiful.

It was a good thought, the selection of Long Island for a military rendezvous, not only for its sanitary merits, but for the security it afforded against desertions. It boasts many fine parade grounds, walks, and lounges, while beautiful views of sea and land greet the eye in every direction. It is of easy communication with the city. I repeat, its selection was a wise idea — a happy accident in the councils of our city *Solons*. Our removal from Faneuil Hall to Long Island was a glorious change. The close, cramped quarters at the hall, with the natural accumulation of filth incidental to the garrisoning of a large number of recruits, rendered still more so by the crowds of visitors who were continually besieging the doors for admittance to see their gallant friends before their departure for the seat of war, from this to the bright sunshine, green fields, and an unimpeded view from the lofty rising ground over an uninterrupted expanse of sea, with capital places for sea-bathing, rendered the change one of special congratulation.

We started from Faneuil Hall early in May, 1861, having previously despatched engineers to lay out the camp, which, at that time, seemed a formidable arrangement; though now it is scarcely five minutes work, then it was five hours. The regiment was there quartered in wall tents, and even with those comfortable accommodations they were not well satisfied (though they have since been glad of the shelter of a few boards, and the lucky possessor of an overcoat, or rubber blanket, thought himself extremely well protected). Having taken possession of their new quarters, the Ninth Regiment, for the first time, considered themselves soldiers.

Immediately upon the arrival of the regiment at Long Island, Colonel Cass assumed control, and it soon became evident to him and his officers, that to make the regiment a good one, and worthy of its distinctive character, a large amount of work must be gone through, and the strictest system of discipline maintained. More than any other man, Colonel Cass knew this. He thoroughly understood the elements of the organization of the men he had to command, and with this knowledge he used the best method of control and instruction. The men were at once instructed in the formula of guard and picket duties, whilst regimental lines were formed, through which none could pass without the countersign or other proper authority. A picket was thrown out around the island, to prevent desertion by boats, or the advent on the island of pleasure parties, without proper authority to land. The strictest surveillance was then maintained over the men, and in a short time the island presented the appearance of a regular military post.

Colonel Cass, though not then proficient in military science, gave, thus early in his military career, evidence of fine soldierly qualities, which, with cultivation, promised noble fruit. The regimental discipline experienced by the men, was also felt by the officers, until at length the spirit which animated the commander extended itself throughout the entire regiment, and soon all joined in the various duties apportioned to them with a hearty good will and spirit, which prognosticated a glorious future — a promise which has since been nobly and gallantly fulfilled.

Company drills took place at stated hours, and in the afternoon battalion drills, under the supervision of Colonel Cass, gradually, yet surely, developed the soldierly qualities of the men. In no camp in the State of Massachusetts could there be found a more hearty desire, or a regiment who worked more strenuously to achieve military perfection than the Ninth. This is vouched for by the citizens of Boston, who on many occasions assembled to witness our drills, when they often expressed themselves greatly gratified and astonished at the extraordinary proficiency of the men, and the rapidity with which they acquired, in so short a time, knowledge of the manual of arms.

Sunday was always a gala day with us at Long Island, visitors being allowed free access, thronged the grounds, seeking among the quarters for husbands, sons, brothers, sweethearts, and friends; bearing with them refreshments and edibles of all kinds, and vying with each other how to express the deep love they bore their gallant defenders, from whom they were soon to be separated, and many of whom were destined to lay down their lives in defence of the nation. On these days would fathers and mothers seek their sons; wives their husbands; sisters their brothers; while, leaning on the arm of some stalwart lover might be seen one of the daughters of Erin's Isle, with blushing cheeks, fit representatives of that loveliness of which authors have written and poets sung, — planning their future after his return, or walking silently with tearful eyes, her heart swelling with love, yet smothering with care the agony she feels at his departure, fearful, lest her despair should cause him a moment's regret.

But the self-sacrificing mother, with a glow of matronly pride upon her cheeks, gazed with unspeakable affection upon her son, or smiled upon him, though her heart shed silent tears, brave in her self-abnegation, for, though language could not tell the strength of her affection, she would not have him stay when her adopted country called him forth to the defence of its honor and its flag! This was a picture that could be witnessed in almost every group. The Irish mother, in this the time of the Union's danger, exemplified the glorious spirit which animated the mothers of Limerick, when their valor hurled back the legions of Prince William, as he vainly strove to destroy the dearly-prized liberty of its people.

It is a proud reflection of the Irishman of this generation, that, when the fidelity of his people was tested, their allegiance was as good a guarantee as birth and native blood to the nation which had trusted in and protected them.

We cannot revert to the delightful reunions of that island camp, the introductory step to the glory which has since crowned our arms, without feelings of deep regret — regret that its companionships and pleasures, its meetings and its partings, may never again be renewed; that we may never again hear the fervent utterings of love from the fond mother and sister; from the cherished wife, and the dear girl whose life was in her love; from the stern father, who feared he would never again grasp the hand of his son; from the brother, undemonstrative in his affection, but with a great wealth of feeling in his heart, — such earnest love is only expressed once in a lifetime, and is born of the peculiar circumstances by which the loved ones are surrounded.

This brief sketch of our island camp may be sufficient to revive, in the minds of those who have visited it, many of the pleasant scenes which transpired there, and the associations connected therewith. Many a brave man has bid it farewell forever! A southern sun blazes down upon his unburied bones; and bleaching skeletons of many of the "Old Ninth" alone remain of those who were once the life of our circle and the brave companions of our battles. To the bereaved ones we would say, for their consolation, Faithful to the cause they joined, they fell; your honor they nobly defended; the country's cause and liberty they valiantly asserted, and died true men and soldiers!

CHAPTER III.

Social Parties. — The Valiant Sentinel. — Plain, plain Tom.

SHADE of Bacchus (if that mythological enormity will condescend us a reflex), what convivial times we had! Deep into the night, and oftentimes to the stilly morn, when the feast of reason and the flow of soul brought forgetfulness of petty cares, and gradually indoctrinated us into the creed of the soldier, that to live, we must live to-day, for a soldier dies to-morrow!

And right willingly we believed in this creed, the truth of which we have seen exemplified on many a bloody field, where the living of yesterday were among the dead of to-day.

In one of our old wall tents the officers would often assemble, and, with a zest that would rival the Irish soldier of the olden time, vent their genial witticisms, perpetrate their jokes, and unwind everlasting yarns, which, if without point, would be certainly brimful of genuine Irish humor. These parties would be, in spirit and feeling, seen all over the camp, and friendships were made and connections formed which will only terminate with life.

These happy parties, however, have been sometimes unceremoniously broken up in the Ninth Regiment, and often have we sprung up from the festive board, drinking the last glass together for a time, and the next moment be sternly dashing into battle, doing our *devoir* for the unity of our adopted country.

Many a vacant seat was there when all was over; but nothing could dampen the ardor of an Irish soldier, and while he spoke a word of sympathy for the dead, he would remark, " It may be my turn to-morrow "— words sometimes only too prophetic.

Many a ludicrous incident occurred at Long Island during our sojourn. I remember well, one evening, that a party of officers sallied out on what we appropriately termed a tour of inspection, ostensibly to visit the guard, but really to pass them, if possible, and visit the camp of another regiment, quartered at the south end of the island. The night was dark, and as we approached the sentinel, we could hear his measured pace; a little nearer, and we heard him pause upon his beat; another moment, and the liquid brogue of the sentinel rang out upon the air, —

"Halt! Who goes there?"

"A friend, with the countersign," was the reply. The sentinel paused, seemingly in meditation: at last a bright idea seemed to strike him, and he cried out, —

"Hold on; ye can't pass here till ye say 'Schouler.'"

We listened with smothered laughter, and then advanced, said "Schouler," and the innocent, good fellow allowed us to pass. *That* was at Long Island, and the soldier was a recruit.

Woe to the man that pressed an advance on the same soldier on the peninsula: a failure to give the proper countersign would be replied to by an ounce of lead. *Then* the soldier was a veteran. At another time, as I was passing from the camp to the boats to take a trip to the city, I espied a stout, heavy fellow, of ponderous proportions, in the full dress of a first-lieutenant. He carried a valise in his hand, and the perspiration ran in rivulets down the creases of his fat physiognomy, and he seemed laboring under serious affliction. He was a comical-looking gentleman, and I paused to survey him more narrowly, when a soldier, who happened to be standing near, irreverently bawled out, "Hollo, Tom! yer off!" The solid gentleman laid his valise upon the ground, and wiping his streaming forehead with a large bandanna, plaintively said, "There it is: a half hour ago it was Lieutenant R——, and now it's *plain, plain Tom!*" It seemed that his commission had been revoked on account of his inability to execute the double-quick movement, which is really a bothersome affair, especially to fat old gentlemen. The soldier knew this, and of the pride Lieutenant R—— derived from his title; therefore it was why the malicious fellow addressed him as plain *Tom*.

"Plain, plain, Tom!" Page 34.

CHAPTER IV.

Leaving Long Island. — A False Alarm. — Arrival at Washington. — Emmart's Farm. — The Captain and his Dog; or, Discipline versus Sagacity.

ON the morning of June 24, 1861, the Ninth Regiment Massachusetts Volunteers embarked on the Ben de Ford, Pembroke, and Cambridge, three large government transports, and in the presence of an immense assemblage, took their departure from Long Island for the city of Washington. On the third day of the passage considerable excitement was manifested, from the fact that it was expected we should be shelled passing the coast of Virginia, at a place called *Matthias Point*, where, it was authoritatively stated, the rebels had planted a masked battery, with which to render unnavigable the waters of the Potomac.

The excitement was increased by the commander of the Quaker City, a United States man-of-war, cruising the Potomac, which had hailed us on the evening of the second day, instructing us to keep a sharp lookout, as, no doubt, we should be attacked passing this point. The only armament aboard the transports was three brass swivel guns of light calibre, of which each vessel had one. An understanding was also had between Colonel Cass and the commander of the Ben de Ford, that, if attacked, he (Cass) would man the boats and storm the batteries, if they opened fire, under the protection of the guns of the transports. Upon approaching the point, the eyes of every officer were bent upon the land with looks of eager expectation, and more than one heart anxiously longed to hear the guns of the battery, that they might have the pleasure of silencing them.

The men had, upon nearing the point, been ordered below, so that the decks were clear for action, and if swept by the enemy's fire, little damage could be done them. The colonel and his officers, with the commanders of the boats, alone remained on the decks. The guns were shotted, and the noble vessels proceeded proudly on their way, and arrived in a short time opposite the Point. Not a sound was heard; not a movement indicated the position where the battery was concealed. In a few minutes the vessels had passed the Point, and no demonstration had been made. It is impossible to say what would have been the result if the battery had opened fire upon us. That an attempt to storm it would have been made we feel quite certain; but experience has since shown us that it might have been a very disastrous undertaking; for, from the nature of the embankment it would be next to impossible to land; and if musketry fire had been used against us, the consequences would have been fearful. After we had passed the fabled monster, and cleared a sufficient interval, the little brass gun of the Ben de Ford blazed forth an indignant challenge, the captain feeling that the security of his position warranted that token of his contempt.

Nothing of interest transpired during the rest of the voyage, except that we lost one man, a young fellow, named Garland, for whom all were sincerely sorry; he fell overboard, and though every effort was made to save him, the darkness of the night rendered our endeavors to help and save fruitless.

The accommodation on board the transports was of the first order; and though we should have preferred to go by rail, still, everything considered, the method of transportation was eminently successful and satisfactory.

On the afternoon of June 29, the transports arrived at the Arsenal wharf at Washington, when the troops disembarked, making their quarters temporarily in the Arsenal yard. Here we lay in our blankets until the morning of the 30th of June, when, after despatching our breakfast, we took up our line of march for the pleasant locality of Emmart's farm, about three miles outside of the city of Washington, where we arrived the same day, and at once pitched our camp.

Emmart's farm proved, eventually, a very excellent place; the mutual understanding between all parties increased, and soon we had a continuation of the genial reunions so auspiciously begun at Long Island.

A number of comical incidents transpired here, one of which I cannot recall without a smile.

We have stated that Colonel Cass was a rigid disciplinarian. This, in truth, he was; so much so, that an officer could not sleep a moment after "*reveille*" without a visit from the colonel, and a gentle reminder that it was time to be up.

One morning, about five o'clock, the writer,

while in silent and close communication with Morpheus, was roughly shaken from his slumbers, and a sharp voice greeted him as he opened his eyes: "Come, you're a pretty fellow; isn't it time for you to be up?" I turned over, and beheld the grim colonel of the regiment and Lieutenant-Colonel Rowell standing solemnly by the bedside, and looking grave as the tomb. "All right, colonel," said I; "I'll get up in a few moments." "See that you do so;" said he, and then he took his departure. Now I should have entered into another arrangement with the mythological god, but that I thought it my duty to warn my comrades of the colonel's presence; therefore I sprang from my couch, consisting of blankets and rails, donned my clothes, and passed outside my tent. As I did so, I glanced up the tented street, and, to my astonishment, beheld the grave and dignified colonel hopping about in the strangest manner, and cutting up the queerest kind of antics, none of which I have ever seen set down in the military books. I went to the rear of one of the tents, to see more clearly what the colonel was doing, and found he was exercising himself in front of Captain Madigan's tent.

It was a comical scene. The colonel would

cautiously approach the door of the tent, and then spring hastily back, while the lieutenant-colonel stood by convulsed with laughter. This manœuvre he executed several times with eminent success, until at last he cried out, "Captain Madigan, Captain Madigan!" He called several times, but the captain did not respond. "I think he's up and out," said Rowell. Cass paused for a moment, and then, muttering anathemas under his breath, strode hastily away. I then moved cautiously towards the tent, to ascertain the cause of the colonel's excitement, and there I beheld Madigan's great bull-dog, which he had brought from Boston, tied to the tent-pole, and growling savagely.

The dog and I were old friends. I patted him on the head, and looked into the tent, and beheld the jolly captain "en deshabille," sitting on a stool, shaking with impressible laughter. He had witnessed the colonel's vain attempt to pass the savage sentinel, and it was as much as he could do to keep from betraying himself.

A few minutes afterwards Captain Madigan met Colonel Cass, and courteously bade him good morning. The colonel looked at him for a moment, and then, with a grim smile, said,

"Madigan, that infernal dog of yours saved you this time; but again, I'll rip open the back of your tent. So now, captain, take care." Madigan was a diplomat, and his only reply was, introducing the colonel to a very nice article which had just come from home.

CHAPTER V.

Summary Treatment of Poachers. — An Unfortunate Rencontre. — Our Valiant Pickets, Pedlers, and Hawkers. — Rumors of a Move. — Bull Run. — Our Night March, and speedy Return to Camp.

THOUGH close to the city of Washington, picket duty was strictly performed by the regiment, the lines extending about a mile from camp, the reserve being stationed near the house of the Washington banker Cochrane, a large and splendid mansion, on the right of Emmart's farm, in a semicircle of dense woods; and never was wood more thoroughly searched than that one, which daily underwent a clean scouring, the commanders of regiments, in the innocence of inexperience, thinking it the secret depository of rebel guns, and the general headquarters of the big spirits of the rebellion!

The residents in that vicinity treated our soldiers with the greatest kindness; and, in return, their property was carefully guarded, and their rights as citizens duly respected. One of the principal reasons which led us to suspect the near vicinage of traitors, was the shooting of two of the New York Fire Zouave regiment, which occurred in the grounds of Mr. ———, who resided near the house of Mr. Cochrane. It was afterwards ascertained that they had been committing depredations on the property one night, and the owner, not knowing them to be soldiers, shot them — a fate which they richly merited.

One morning, shortly after the arrival of the regiments at Emmart's farm, an officer was with his company, engaged in drill, and in passing a belt of wood, two shots were fired in rapid succession, and two of the men fell, one wounded in the leg, and the other in the shoulder. Two men were sent into the wood, but soon returned, stating that they could see no one, and giving it as their opinion, that the shots had come from the other side of the wood, from the camp of the Twenty-seventh New York Volunteers (Germans), who were out at target practice. As this seemed the most reasonable view to be taken of the case, the officer marched his company back to camp, and reported the affair to the colonel. But Colonel Cass would not divest his mind of the idea that the shots had been fired by rebel scouts, and as the colonel was looked upon by the regiment as the embodiment of military wisdom, his opinion was favorably received, and caused considerable excitement. Before we left that camp, however, the colonel was compelled to acknowledge, that if we desired to find rebels, we must move forward several miles, cross the Potomac, and picket the enemy's territory — a movement we shortly afterwards made.

Our regiment greatly improved in discipline while encamped at Emmart's farm, and became much more conversant with picket duty, so that, in a little while, a pig or cow *might* pass them, perhaps, in the dark, without receiving a bullet in its brain for refusing to answer the "challenge;" though I must confess that when the Ninth had seen some service, and consequently were more accurate in their aim, when a pig passed them they seldom cried, "Who goes there?" but with malice *prepence* "nailed" the unfortunate porker without a word.

Every suspicious-looking individual in the vicinity of our camp, and every pedler, male or female, were unceremoniously seized by our patriotic fellows as spies, and transferred from department to department, until, finally, after having "gone the rounds," the unfortunate individuals found themselves, several weeks after, pursuing the same humble but honest occupation, in the same place, in the same clothes, and, seemingly, with the same vendible stock of goods, but *this* time under the safeguard of a pass. One cannot look back to these days of military verdancy without a smile. We, the scarcely fledged children of Mars, believed in the omnipotence of the sword, and had no sooner shed our citizen's coat than we looked with suspicion and distrust on every one who twirled canes, when, instead, we thought they should be manipulating muskets. These feelings and fancies, however, are natural to the opening career of the Republican soldier, and are easily eradicated by experience. The veteran looks back to them with mingled feelings of pride and mortification; therefore it is, that in the conduct of the American soldier there is nothing arbitrary or tyrannical; with experience he dismounts from his stilts, and never strives to reach an unbecoming altitude again.

The monotony of our life at Emmart's farm was soon destined to be relieved, for, upon the evening of July 20, 1861, orders reached our camp for the troops to be in readiness to move at a moment's notice, with three days' rations in our haversacks. Orderlies and staff officers could be seen riding rapidly in the direction of every regiment in our vicinity, and a very large force was encamped immediately around, for hours before we received our marching orders. Regiment after regiment were under arms, and soon defiling past our camp, — stately columns so soon to be sundered, broken, and beaten; fresh, noble soldiers, soon to be weary, dispirited, and defeated, — passed us all the afternoon, and the last regiment we saw march away was the Second New Hampshire.

The camp was rife with rumors. A great battle was soon to be fought, or was already in progress. Little we knew that the terrible and disastrous field of Bull Run was already lost to our arms, and that our magnificent legions were even then flying before a victorious foe.

Rapidly the Second New Hampshire defiled from the camp, and the sun was already disappearing behind the hills when the left of the regiment passed from view. Anxiously the Ninth, standing armed and equipped in their company streets, awaited the order to march.

Our brave, muscular fellows seemed animated with deep enthusiasm; an intense longing to meet the foe pervaded their breasts. Their nostrils seemed to scent the blood of their dying countrymen as it poured vainly on the battlefield; and yet this enthusiasm was not vented in shouts and cheers, but exhibited in the alacrity which animated their movements; in the firm, solid grasp of their weapons; in the rapid obedience to orders as rapidly given; in the patience with which, when everything was ready, they awaited the order to move. Night was upon us when the order came. It was received with one wild, ringing cheer, and in another moment the shadowy outline of the soldiers could be seen moving swiftly from the camp. We marched fast until late into the night, with the full conviction that on the morrow we should fight,— when, suddenly, a staff-officer halted the regiment, and desired to speak to Colonel Cass.

The result of this communication was, that the regiment "about faced," and we marched back to our old camp by the light of the moon, filled with chagrin and disappointment. The regiment was then formed in square, and Colonel Cass expressed to them his heartiest approval, and the pride he felt in commanding such men, whose alacrity and enthusiasm in marching to the field fully verified his most sanguine expectations. Well might Colonel Cass feel proud of such men. Their valor has shed glory on his name, on the land of their birth, and that of their adoption. The regiment was then marched to quarters, and in a little while the whole command was buried in sleep. The regiments which had marched away earlier in the day did not return. Had Colonel Cass received the order a few hours earlier, the Ninth would have been precipitated into the disastrous battle of Bull Run, and, though they might have shared the general defeat, they would have valiantly responded to the despairing cry of the immortal Sixty-ninth, "Where, O, where, is the Irish Ninth?"

CHAPTER VI.

Our retreating Forces. — Scenes on the Way. — We march for Arlington. — Our gratifying Reception.

THE gloomy morning of Monday, July 22, broke upon us. The sky, heavy and dark with clouds, opened its reservoirs of rain, which poured down without cessation, everything around looking dark and dismal. The rain pattered down upon our canvas houses until the very sound became irksome; as a relief, we went out into the storm, and after getting well saturated, visited the quarters of Lieutenant Tobin, and in company with him and Captain Madigan, went down to the camp lately occupied by the Second New Hampshire.

We expected to see no one there, and were surprised when we learned that Captain S—— and some other officers of that regiment had just arrived. We called at his quarters, and there learned of the terrible defeat our arms had experienced. Captain S—— gave us a detailed account of that most fearful rout, and portrayed, in graphic language, the terrible scenes to be witnessed on the road to Centreville and towards Washington — wagon trains deserted and destroyed; supplies of all kinds recklessly flung away; wounded men stretched about on every hand, under the furious pelting of the pitiless storm, no one to care for them; fugitives, half clad, without muskets or equipments of any kind, their faces expressing the terror that ran riot in their hearts; weapons, whole and broken, lying by the road-side, the only idea animating the flying and frightened men being escape from the victors — the broken wagons and dead horses pointing the road to the capital. In Washington itself the excitement was fearful — the inhabitants fleeing to every place of security in their consternation; wearied soldiers sleeping upon the sidewalks, the curbstones for their pillow, and the rain pouring in torrents upon them; the streets filled with broken wagons; stores with doors flung open, no one to protect the goods nor any to steal them; the very heads of the nation aghast at the magnitude of their misfortune, and the whole system of the government for a time impotent and paralyzed. This solemn news fell upon our ears that fatal Monday morning. Turning round, we beheld the fugitives dragging their tired limbs towards the camps; some, who had been shot through the cheek and other parts of the head and body, wretchedly bandaged: men maimed in every conceivable manner, weak, spiritless, and broken down, were there, slowly and painfully wending their weary way. It was a terrible picture of incompetency and disgrace, and we turned away, sick at heart, and felt thankful that the Ninth was still the perfect regiment that came from home, and that its virgin colors were not stained by any sign of defeat.

For a while our hearts were heavy as we gazed on the sad picture spread out before us, and we could scarcely reconcile the thought that these men had yesterday marched past us, strong, valiant, with the flush of hope and pride beaming on their manly cheeks, so worn, wretched-looking, and despairing did they now appear! But only for a while were our hearts heavy: the sun broke through the black clouds; the rain ceased to fall, and as we reached our camp we saw our regiment in line. That splendid array of men in all the glorious paraphernalia of war, firm, self-reliant, and cheerful, struck us with admiration. We thought no longer of the fugitives; we harbored no more pictures of despair; and as we gazed upon our green flag, side by side with the starry banner, — the sunburst and the eagle, — we felt that victory would crown the nation's arms, and shed her glory upon the Ninth.

The result of the battle of Bull Run did not in the least affect the spirits of our regiment. "Send us against them, and we'll turn the tide; we'd whip them to submission, if only half supported," were the remarks they made; and they performed their duties with the same alacrity and cheerfulness as if the battle of Bull Run had never been fought.

The nation rapidly recovered from the effects of that disastrous battle, and made immediate preparations for strengthening the defences of the capital, which caused the Ninth Regiment again to receive marching orders, which came on the morning of July 23. At an early hour tents were struck, baggage wagons loaded, and the regiment on the road. We marched through Washington late in the afternoon, crossed the Potomac, and moved directly to that part of

Arlington known as the "Lee estate," which then belonged to the commander-in-chief of the Confederate forces. Night came on as we continued our march; and as we moved along the roads and through the woods, our progress was hailed with loud cheers from regiments encamped on our line of march and immense bonfires had been prepared for our reception, as the fame of the Irish Ninth had preceded us. These fires extended along the whole route to Arlington, some being in dense woods, only visible through one grand opening where the regiments were encamped, and presented a spectacle most sublime. The forms of men reflected in the red light of the fires, the clash and glitter of arms, the loud shouts of welcome, and every conceivable expression of enthusiasm, made the scene alike grand and affecting. The route to Arlington was one grand ovation; and as we left the gallant regiments behind, we could hear, floating upon the night wind, the ghostly echo of, "Three cheers for the Ninth!" Our men were delighted and surprised, proud to know that thus early their merits as Irishmen and gallant soldiers were recognized. As they marched along, their tread became more determined; their columns seemed more compact, and satisfaction gleamed on every countenance.

At a late hour we halted in a wood at the rear of Arlington House (Lee's mansion), where, fires being lighted, we made a hasty supper, and, spreading our blankets, soon in sleep forgot the fatigues of the day.

CHAPTER VII.

Arlington. — General Lee's House. — A Negress. — How Lee kept a dying Wish. — A good Breakfast. — Negroes and Negro Minstrels. — We resume our March.

WE awoke from the enjoyment of a most comfortable night's sleep to behold the sun glimmering in through the interstices of the trees, and to hear the birds chirping their morning melodies from the branches above our heads. It was early morning, and scarcely any one had risen, for the bugle had not yet sounded the reveille, and until its ringing blast is heard by the soldier, he will sleep on and on, until, like Rip Van Winkle, he wakes in another age, and looks around him upon other scenes. A few of the officers had risen, drawn from their blankets by the beauty of the morning; and, in imitation of these admirers of nature, we arose and joined them, when it was proposed that a search should be made for some habitation, where, by the expenditure of a few dimes, we might achieve the matutinal meal.. This weighty and important proposition, having been duly considered, was adopted, and in a few moments we were working our way along a footpath through the wood, which, we sincerely trusted, would lead to some "local habitation," we cared not whether with or without a name. We followed the path for some distance, and suddenly found ourselves on the verge of the wood, and directly before us a large, solid, square-looking building, architecturally plain, the surface covered with a kind of rough cement. There was nothing inviting in the appearance of the building, but the scenery by which it was surrounded at once filled us with admiration.

It stood upon a high hill, from the base of which ran undulating valleys, dotted here and there with patches of green wood, and likewise interspersed with rich fields in an advanced state of cultivation. The view from the front of the mansion was supremely beautiful, the scenery being the only pleasing characteristic. The house itself looked more like a huge public building than the residence of a private gentleman.

From the building itself we turned our attention to a group of small, wooden houses, of a very dilapidated appearance. They had, at some anterior period of their history, received a careless whitewashing, patches of which, scattered here and there, alone remained. At the door of one of these houses stood an ancient negro — ancient in aspect, ancient in dress, ancient in his method of speech, with a very ancient stick in his hand, in an attitude of meditation.

We courteously accosted him, and asked if he resided there. He told us that he did, and was a farm hand of Massa Lee's (since General R. E. Lee). We learned from him that he had been a slave from boyhood in the Lee family, and had passed nearly all his life on that estate. In the course of conversation, he informed us that General Lee was very arbitrary with his slaves, and recognized no rights of theirs, and further told us that the "gal" over the way — pointing to another of the wooden houses — would have been free upon the death of a certain Mrs. Custis, but that, although it was her dying wish, General Lee, notwithstanding he had consented to her wishes *before* her death, absolutely refused to recognize them on being called upon to do so after her decease; so the girl had ever since remained a slave. The old negro enumerated many other of the general's characteristics, which, in our opinion, did not redound to his (General Lee's) honor or humanity. We left the old man, and went to the "house over the way," and saw the "gal" referred to, — a strapping wench, about thirty-five years old, — and her husband a man about the same age. They invited us to take a seat, with which invitation we complied; and as a warm and very enticing breakfast was upon the table, we suggested the propriety of partaking of it, and under the influence of several glittering silver quarter dollars, they very cordially acquiesced. A tender steak, beautiful yellow butter, spread plentifully upon nice corn-cake, rich cream submerged in a cup of delicious coffee, sharpened with witty and genial conversation, — for which the officers of the Ninth are proverbial, — these were the component parts of that memorable breakfast. The negress narrated that phase of her misfortune referred to by the old negro without, and while she eulogized the memory of her "dear departed mistress," she anathematized, without stint, the treacherous and dishonorable conduct of General Lee; who, she said, "would never be concerned with anything good, and if he was, it would be sure to go to the bad." She was very intelligent, and had none of that idiom so unsparingly used by the so-called "minstrels" when delineating negro life and character. In fact, though we have seen nearly all kinds of negroes, and have had a genuine plantation boy in our own service, we have never yet met with any who can approach the absurdities, in action, feature, or distorted language, so unsparingly thrust upon the general public by these pseudo darkies. We remained in conversation there some time, and when our drums sounded, came away with a very bad opinion of the moral character of General Lee, however great our admiration may be respecting his military abilities.

We marched from the grounds of the Lee estate, about ten o'clock on the morning of the 23d, to that part of Arlington Heights where that noble monument of Irish energy and industry stands in frowning might, — Fort Corcoran, — where, after a slow and weary march over bad roads, we arrived about five o'clock, halted, and camped for the night a short distance from the Heights, on the hill fronting the Fort, and went to sleep, highly pleased with our reception by the forces of Colonel, afterwards Brigadier-General Corcoran, who thronged the roads and cheered us on our way to camp.

CHAPTER VIII.

We occupy the Heights.—Fort Cass.—The Cow Bell.—Pleasant Society.—"Balls Hamilton."—We are presented with Colors.—McClellan organizes the Army.—Grand Review.

AT an early hour next morning a number of men were detailed to proceed to the Heights and clear a sufficient space in the dense woods for camping purposes. A few hours' labor and it was done. About noon the tents of the different companies were pitched, roads from the camp to the main road cut, and a bridge constructed under the superintendence of Lieutenant-Colonel Rowell. The bridge was named after him, and still exists. After laboring the whole day to perfect the camp, the men, who were pretty well tired out with marching and hard work, retired to their quarters, and slept comfortably and soundly till morning. Next day the usual duties of a camp were resumed, and the regiment, with the exception of those retained for camp guard and picket duty, commenced to clear the wood preparatory to forming an *abatis* on our front, to obstruct the passage of the enemy's cavalry should they succeed in forcing our pickets. About this time picket duty was becoming a serious affair, the rebels being in force about two or three miles on our front, having a large camp of infantry and cavalry in the immediate vicinity of Falls' Church. The utmost vigilance had to be maintained in order to secure us from the enemy's incursions; but by this time our men were thoroughly posted in their various duties, and we anticipated good and vigilant service.

It took but a short time to complete the *abatis* upon our front and flank; and when this was done, a new and more stupendous work presented itself, which was no less than the erection of a large fort on our left, constructed to mount five guns. To green troops this was no ordinary undertaking; but the officers and men entered into the work with great spirit; space for a magazine was cleared; the breastworks gradually arose; the embrasures speedily appeared; then quarters for officers and men; till, in the space of two months, that noble work now known as "Fort Cass," in memory of our lamented and gallant colonel, arose in frowning defiance — one of the strongest defences upon that side of the Potomac. It is a lasting monument of industry (being completed in less than six weeks) and mechanical skill, and will bear lasting credit to our gallant and industrious soldiers. A detachment from our own regiment garrisoned the fort for a few weeks, when, after it was fully mounted and thoroughly completed, it was turned over to a Wisconsin regiment, which permanently garrisoned it. These were the principal labors of the Ninth while at Arlington Heights; and we are glad to say, they received the highest encomium from the general officers of the divisions, and the regiment was highly complimented for the engineering skill which it exhibited.

While encamped at Arlington the usual number of practical jokes were perpetrated; convivial parties convened, as at our other camps; but it was here that, for the first time, streets were named, and particular messes donned the most peculiar cognomens. The "Cow Bell," or "Our Mess," situated in Company C's Street, was the headquarters of the wags and practical jokers. There Captain Madigan flourished, a wit and every inch a gentleman; a brave soldier, who perished gallantly fighting, at the battle of the Chickahominy. Madigan was a punster and a vocalist; could tell a pleasing story, or perpetrate a good joke. He was greatly beloved by his brother officers, and his death, noble and patriotic though it was, filled them with profound sorrow. Lieutenant Ned McSweeney was another member of the "Cow Bell,"— a dashing, handsome young officer,— and the life of our circle. He fell bravely fighting at Malvern Hill. His name is well preserved in the regiment, and he will ever be remembered for his genial qualities. Lieutenant John Rafferty, as brave, generous, open-hearted a man as ever drew a sword, has often made the "Cow Bell" ring with laughter at his quaint humor and pleasant stories. He was full of eccentric notions. He, too, is with the gallant dead,— struck down in his prime, in the midst of battle, on Malvern Hill; but he leaves behind him a memory which is proudly cherished by his comrades, who mourn his glorious, but, alas! too speedy end. Three out of the six members of the "Cow Bell" mess alone remain — we among them. But a halo of glory surrounds the memory of those who are gone,—

> "There's a tear for all that die,
> A mourner o'er the humblest grave;
> *But nations swell the funeral cry,*
> *And triumph weeps above the brave."*

The furious battles of the peninsula depleted many a joyful mess, left many a vacant chair. The tent that resounded with jocund mirth to-night would be silent and lonely to-morrow.

Among the men, some of the tents rejoiced in names expressive, humorous, and even diabolical. One company had, among others, one called "The Devil's Kitchen;" and from the loud conviviality which at times emanated from it, we would almost conclude that his Satanic majesty was the president of the assemblage.

One of the many comical characters attached to our regiment was "Balls Hamilton;" and he, indeed, was a comical guy. When he first called on Captain Madigan, he stated to him that he had been told that he (Captain Madigan) commanded the "colored" company, and that he was desirous of being servant to the commander. Madigan told him that he did indeed command the color company, and if he wished to join, he might do so, first getting the consent of the chaplain, whose servant he (Balls) then was.

Balls was too comical a character for the

worthy father, and he readily gained his consent to attach himself to the "colored company."

Great was Hamilton's astonishment when he found the members of the "colored company" were as white as the rest of the regiment. The reader will readily understand the black boy's mistake; the company always carried the colors of the regiment, and were therefore called the "color" company. Hamilton, however, soon recovered from his disappointment, and occupies a prominent part in a large picture of the "Cow Bell," by Brady, in which appear all the members of that famous mess — the dead and the living. In the picture Hamilton is "passant" upon the ground, with the long, thin sword of a sergeant in his hand; an expression of "beautiful serenity" is upon his face, derived, principally, from the expansion of his tremendous mouth, and the comical roll of his immense eyes. He looked so warlike, with the sword in his hand, that we afterwards christened him "Toussaint L'Ouverture;" in fact, we imagined him a fair resemblance of that distinguished character. Mr. "Balls Hamilton" remained with the mess a long time. He was originally hired as cook, in which capacity he officiated for a few days, and was so "remarkably expeditious" in his profession that we concluded it would be preferable to detail a white man to supply his place. This was done; and in a few days "Balls" proved himself more competent to *superintend* the white cook than to perform the labors himself.

Poor Madigan! How he would make that old mess tent ring with the favorite drinking song, —

> "Come, let every old bachelor fill up his glass,
> Vive la compagnie!
> And drink to the health of his favorite lass;
> Vive la compagnie!

Then rolled out a medley of voices, —

> "Vive la, vive la, vive l'amour,
> Vive l'amour,
> Vive l'amour,
> Vive la compagnie!"

We cannot look back upon the history of our regiment without recalling these pleasant scenes.

The few that remain of our original regiment will look back with emotion to the hills of Arlington, where they graduated as soldiers, and from whence they went forth to work out their desperate and bloody future upon the peninsula;

where, among the great of the magnificent army of the Potomac, they were held in warm esteem, and always occupied the front position.

There we received from the boys of the *Eliot School* that distinguished mark of their young regard, — the national flag, — which led us into every battle we were engaged in on the peninsula, and in defending which many standard-bearers fell, notwithstanding, it always fluttered proudly in the front of the fight, side by side with our "Irish green." If our gallant fellows faltered before the desperate onslaught of the enemy, the cry, "Rally round the green flag, boys!" brought them together; and, with a genuine Irish cheer, they would dash down upon the foe, hurling him back with superhuman strength.

The organization of the army of the Potomac was commenced at Arlington, in and around which, the "grand army" was encamped, under the military supervision of General George B. McClellan. Order came from chaos; brigades, divisions, and grand divisions sprang into existence, and with them the different departments necessary to pay, clothe, and feed them. The grand army, though thus divided, was as a unit in all military manœuvres; like a ponderous machine of innumerable parts, it was so cleverly united, that, by the will of one, the whole of the immense fabric could be moved; and this stupendous work of military genius was but the labor of a few weeks; for General McClellan soon understood the qualities of the men at his disposal. He found intelligence, patriotism, and military ardor; his wishes were understood, his plans of organization rapidly effected; and soon, very soon, he had the gratification of presenting to the people of America that mighty indicator of their power, " the grand army of the Potomac."

This achieved, brigade drills and brigade and division reviews became the order of the day, and gradually the perfection of military discipline was attained; the rough wheels of the machine became polished, and soon the gigantic fabric moved with surprising accuracy and unequalled success. At the reviews General McClellan was usually present, and was always received with wild enthusiasm. We shall never forget the grand review of the whole army, which took place at Bailey's Cross Roads, about two miles from Arlington Heights, in August, 1861. It was a most magnificent sight. Nearly a hundred thousand men were under arms, with heads erect, their arms and equipments almost rivalling the sun in brightness; themselves models of cleanliness and uniformity that would have satisfied the most fastidious military critic; everything was regularity, and every movement made with that precision and perfection which is only attained by close attention and observance of good discipline, while their stalwart forms and healthy smiling faces could not fail to gratify the beholder. These were the children of the republic, the devoted sons of the nation, assembled in their might to smite the traitors that would trample on the integrity of its constitution. Never before was such a sight seen upon this broad continent, and, once seen, will never be forgotten.

General McClellan was pleased to compliment our regiment on its appearance on this occasion, with whom he has always enjoyed great popularity.

CHAPTER IX.

We leave Arlington. — Arrive at Miner's Hill. — Painful Scene. — Many killed and wounded. — Colonel Cass' Opinion. — How we kept Christmas. — Lieutenant-Colonel Peard dies. — Fairfax. — A March in the Rain. — Alexandria.

WE left Arlington Heights late in the afternoon of October 29, 1861, leaving the woods all ablaze with innumerable camp fires, presenting a most brilliant pyrotechnic display, and marched in the direction of Miner's Hill, about five miles distant. The roundabout way which we took in marching there consumed a deal of time, and caused a late arrival. We halted near the house of one Basil Hall, stacked arms, and, resting, waited for orders to pitch tents. We had waited about an hour, when the sharp roll of musketry rang out on the night air, and the cries of falling men saluted us from the direction of our right, and about three hundred yards distant. Another and another roll of musketry proclaimed the meeting of opposing forces. Colonel Cass gave the command, "Fall in, lads!" The line officers took up the cry, "Fall in, lads, and lively!" With the calm precision of veteran troops the men took their places behind their guns; and, when the next command, "Take arms," was given, one could scarce hear the rattle of their weapons. The cries of wounded men disturbed the stillness of the night, and told us that considerable havoc had been made by the firing we had heard. The regiment stood patiently awaiting orders, a picket being thrown out on the front and flanks. In a short time the officer of the picket came in with the terrible intelligence that our troops had been firing into each other; that a force of cavalry from the front had, upon meeting the regiment of Colonel Baker (Californian) mistook his command for rebels, and fired upon them. Colonel Baker's regiment had immediately returned the fire. The left of Colonel Baker's brigade had now come up, and mistaking the right for rebels, made the same terrible blunder as the cavalry; they immediately levelled their pieces, and discharged such a terrific volley at their comrades as stretched many a gallant Californian upon the grass. Four batteries of artillery were posted a short distance off, with the intention of sweeping the Californian brigade; and God help the poor fellows if the fuse had been snapped on the cannon, for terrible would have been the havoc committed. However, luckily, they were made aware of the fearful blunder. In an instant the pieces had changed position; in an instant every rifle was lowered, and men kneeling beside the comrade they had just shot, dropping water upon his parched and dying lips, and shedding tears of rage and sorrow. It was a terrible and affecting scene. The cause of this unfortunate affair has never been satisfactorily explained; but General Smith, then commanding that brigade, we think, cannot but feel that the onus of that terrible night's work rests heavily on his shoulders.

The official account given of this extraordinary mistake, we feel safe in stating, did not correspond with the facts as they actually occurred. The names of killed and wounded amounted to many more than were officially reported, and bordered somewhere upon fifty-four killed and wounded. The graves of those killed can still be seen, and the recollection of that fatal night awakens feelings of sympathy and regret.

Such was our solemn introduction to our camp at Miner's Hill, where we remained, doing picket duty, and a variety of labor incidental to a soldier's life in camp. Here we will relate an anecdote characteristic of Colonel Cass, in connection with the unfortunate *rencontre* above referred to. The position of the artillery on that occasion was such that if the Ninth had advanced, they must have received the same politeness shown the Californians. In complimenting Colonel Cass upon the coolness of his regiment in that fearful and trying emergency, General Morell asked him what he would have done if the battery had opened fire upon him. "Done!" exclaimed the colonel, with a flash of his penetrating eye; " I would have charged the battery, and by Heaven I'd have taken it too!" Those who knew Colonel Cass, and the regiment, felt the full force of his remark; and we think, that in the panic which then existed, he would have taken it even if defended by a brigade.

To record many of the events that occurred at Miner's Hill would only be a repetition of former scenes, detailed in previous chapters. Christmas was celebrated there with an *éclat* highly creditable to those concerned. A profusion of luxuries was sent to the regiment from Washington, the camp was splendidly decorated with ivy, evergreens, and arches enclosing appropriate mottos and compliments to distinguished generals of the army. General Fitz-John Porter had been invited, but was unable to attend. In the punning language of the lamented Madigan, 'While we deplored the absence of 'Porter,' we were happily supplied with 'more ale;' the witty reference being to General Morell, who honored the regiment with his presence, accompanied by his staff. The joviality of these Christmas festivities will doubtless be long remembered. Among the guests present on that memorable night were Colonel Woodbury, Fourth Michigan, and Colonel Black, of the Sixty-second Pennsylvania Volunteers — the guests of Colonel Cass and his officers. These three colonels, all of the same brigade, have since died in battle, or from wounds received on the peninsula. No abler commanders were in any brigade in the army of the Potomac.

These festivities were honored by the gratifying presence of several ladies, which greatly enhanced and increased the enjoyment of the festive season.

On the 25th of January, Lieutenant-Colonel Peard died. He was promoted on the discharge of Lieutenant-Colonel Rowell, who had resigned some time previously, and was a good officer, and highly esteemed by the regiment.

Early on the morning of the 10th of March we struck tents; and, while speaking of tents, we may relate an incident connected with them which occurred here. Soon after our arrival at Miner's Hill, our regiment received that kind of small tents called "poncho," and now in general use in the army. The men at that time had "wedge" tents. When the "ponchos" were brought, one of them was put up, near the large tents of the officers for the men to examine. Truly it was a cheerless-looking little affair: the men would look at it, walk round it, look through from one end to the other, then look at the large and commodious tents they then occupied; then they would sadly shake their heads, heave a deep sigh, and walk meditatively away. They could not imagine how a man was to lie inside of it: when they got used to them they found that the same tents would hold three, and sometimes four, on a pinch.

Our line of march lay over roads deeply cut

up by the artillery and wagon trains. Very muddy, and very tired, we reached Fairfax Court House, Virginia, a distance of twelve miles, the men on this march carrying their knapsacks, &c., heavily laden. Here we ascertained, from the cavalry, that Manassas had been evacuated. We remained here some days, awaiting orders, and on the 15th we marched towards Alexandria. It rained fearfully, and nearly all the day we were marching knee-deep in water and mud, and were glad to halt after travelling more than twelve miles, pitching our camp at a place called by some "Camp California," while by others, more appropriately, "Camp Misery."

At reveille in the morning, a waggish sergeant called at the door (?) of every poncho, and asked to be allowed to scrape the shoes of the occupants. The request was novel and surprising, but of course granted with alacrity. The sergeant was careful to put into a great paper bag the combined dirt of five hundred army brogans. Having got back to his headquarters, he closed the bag, and tied it with all the taste and tidiness of a grocer's clerk. His eccentric proceeding was still a mystery to his comrades, some of whom were watching him with a lively curiosity.

The sergeant took his pen, and explained himself by labelling the package, ironically, "The Government Bounty Land of Five Hundred Veteran Volunteers." I dedicate this joke to Congress.

The next day was Sunday, and being a bright, clear day, gave the men a good opportunity to dry their clothes, which it is unnecessary to say they took advantage of. During the day our camp was shifted a few hundred yards back, and directly in front of Fort Worth.

We remained at this place until Friday, the 21st, when, passing through Alexandria, we embarked on board the steamer State of Maine, for Fortress Monroe. On board the transport we found very comfortable and satisfactory arrangements, and started on our voyage, the men of the regiment in the best possible spirits.

CHAPTER X.

Our Bonnie Green Flag. — We reach Hampton, Va. — A Reconnoissance. — We march for Yorktown. — Our Men dig Intrenchments. — The Evacuation of Yorktown. — We start for West Point. — Columbia Landing. — White House. — Gaines' Mills and Hanover Court House. — An Engagement. — A noble Deed.

WHEN the steamer had hauled out into the stream, the general commanding ordered our green flag to be hoisted at the main truck. In a few moments the Irish symbol was run up aloft, and proudly the dear old flag fluttered in the breeze. It seemed like a bird of golden plumage, that had been long imprisoned, and snapped its folds in a sort of triumphant glee. Wild cheers rang out from a thousand Irish throats, and many a tear-dimmed eye gazed on the famous banner as it proudly floated on the air, and, from its glorious altitude, seeming to symbolize poor Ireland's future.

What wild thoughts animated the hearts of those exiled heroes as they gazed upon that flaunting flag, the world will never know; but that glorious moment will never pass from the minds of those that live to keep it cherished in the sanctuary of their memory.

The next day the regiment arrived at Fortress Monroe, and, after disembarking, marched at once to Hampton, Virginia. Nothing of interest occurred upon the route. The next day we changed our camp, to make room for other troops, which were continually arriving, and moved a distance of two miles, to a place in the vicinty of Newmarket Bridge, Virginia.

On the 27th of March the regiment formed part of a grand reconnoissance to Big Bethel, under command of General Porter, where they discovered a nest of rebels about five hundred strong. After a sharp contest, they were driven from their works, leaving their dinners behind them in their hasty flight. The same night we returned to camp, after marching a distance of twenty miles.

Early on the morning of Friday, the 4th of April, the regiment left Hampton, *en route* for Yorktown, throwing out skirmishers during the march. The enemy left their fortifications after firing a few shells. That night we reached

Cockletown, and camped there, having marched about eighteen miles. We were very tired, and soon afterwards all hands gladly lay down and slept.

Early the following day the regiment continued the line of march, and about one o'clock arrived in front of the enemy's works before Yorktown, when they opened fire upon us, doing, however, little or no damage. Companies D and I were thrown out as skirmishers, and advanced to within four hundred yards of the enemy's works, which kept up a heavy and continuous fire. It was not, however, until the enemy opened upon them with some very large guns, casting shell and shot around, that they thought it advisable to retire.

They remained that night in a ravine, close to the enemy's works, and could not pitch their tents, as they would attract attention. The shells throughout the night flew among them rather thick, without, however, doing any harm, though one man was killed and four wounded in the next regiment. General McClellan passed us here for the first time on the peninsula, and was received with great enthusiasm.

On the night of April 6 the Ninth was ordered

out to dig intrenchments close to the enemy's works. The men labored with cautiousness and silence, and fully succeeded in their undertaking. With the morning sun the enemy perceived, to their astonishment and chagrin, a fine intrenchment, with good breastworks, dug out and thrown up under the very muzzles of their guns. They, however, did not seem to appreciate it as well as ourselves, and began shelling us in a "promiscuous" manner. It rained extremely hard the next day, and fifty men from each company in our regiment were detailed for picket duty. This was quite an uncomfortable job; but our lads obeyed the order with alacrity. During the day the firing between our artillery and that of the enemy was pretty heavy, and a large number of our party were killed. A continuous rain extended over that and the whole of the following day, with no prospect of clearing up. The shells from the enemy burst around us on every hand, some close to our regiment, but doing little or no damage. For some days the men were kept very busy at work in the trenches, the enemy firing occasionally, but never deterring our men from the pursuit of their honest avocations. Sometimes in the night we would be aroused from our repose by the loud thunder of the enemy's cannon, and the shriek of shells, that would pass in, over, and around our camp, scattering men and matter with the utmost nonchalance and impunity. The impudence of these shells was unparalleled; there was no mischief they would not do if properly directed; in fact, in the expressive language of "one of ours," "They had more cheek than they could well carry."

Matters continued in this state for a number of days. At three o'clock in the afternoon of Saturday, May 3, 1862, a shell burst close to our camp. It was the last shell sent forth from beleaguered Yorktown. A piece of it, weighing eight pounds, dropped near the right of Company I's street.

At seven o'clock A. M., on Sunday, May 14, a report spread from mouth to mouth, and from camp to camp, that Yorktown was evacuated. The greatest enthusiasm prevailed. The engineering genius of McClellan had overcome all obstacles, and Yorktown had succumbed.

About one o'clock P. M., the same day, we were ordered out, in light marching order, to garrison and guard the forts that were taken.

Shortly after the victorious army of the Potomac was on the march in search of the foe.

At eight o'clock, on that memorable day, our regiment returned to camp, and soon afterwards three days' rations were issued to each man, in preparation for an immediate march; but later we learned, to our great disappointment, that it had been decided to leave our division behind. The night was dark and dismal; the rain poured in torrents. The regiment was expecting to move at a moment's notice, and they waited with great impatience the coming of orders. In the morning heavy firing was heard in the direction of Williamsburg, and it was surmised that our army had reached the rearguard of the retreating forces. About seven o'clock in the evening our division was upon the road, but was immediately ordered back until daylight.

The next morning was beautiful and bracing; the firing had ceased. We were preparing to march, when a rumor reached us that McClellan had captured a thousand prisoners, and was in hopes of a complete victory. In the evening, about eight o'clock, we struck tents, and at midnight moved on Yorktown. After a rapid march the regiment arrived there, and we stretched ourselves upon the ground, and, wrapped in our blankets, slept until morning.

The next day we had an opportunity of visiting the various forts and defences in the immediate vicinity, and could not but admire the engineering skill they exhibited. Then, for the first time, the extraordinary labor of General McClellan could be appreciated. There, before us, stood that monument of the triumph of his engineering skill. Yorktown could have been made to succumb in no other way. Generals of less ability would have attempted the subjugation of the works by storm — a proceeding which would have been attended with terrible disasters, and have culminated in defeat.

The method and plans of General McClellan were those of a wise and humane soldier; and history will eventually decide that, in compelling the evacuation of Yorktown, McClellan achieved one of those rare feats in military history, which will prove the finest laurel in the chaplet that crowns his brow. As we passed, a number of soldiers of various regiments were clustered round and upon the spot where Cornwallis delivered his sword to Washington; and we noticed that many of them broke off pieces of stone and carried them away as "souvenirs" of that memorable surrender.

On the 9th of May we arrived at West Point, Virginia, about two miles from which we encamped for the night, the men here being obliged to sleep on the ground, as their tents had not arrived. But we managed to pass a tolerable night. The next day we moved our camp a short distance. At this time we were about twenty-eight miles from Richmond.

The following day we were again supplied with three days' rations, and had orders to be ready, in light marching order, to move on Richmond. The graves of Union and rebel soldiers are scattered plentifully about West Point, and tell of the vigor of the fighting at that place. Next day General McClellan, happening to pass by where our regiment lay, our boys loudly cheered him, which was continued by other regiments as he passed on the road.

We remained here about two days, when we received orders to draw five days' rations, and to have one day's ration cooked, and be ready to move at two o'clock the following morning, when we struck tents, and about half past four were on our line of march.

The reader will, no doubt, perceive how rigorous and unceasing was the work of the last few weeks. But he cannot comprehend the innumerable difficulties with which we had to contend; the many comfortless nights we passed without shelter, in the midst of storm and rain, marching ankle-deep in mud and water, and lying down at night on a couch composed of that cold but plastic compound.

However, the thought that Richmond was to fall before our conquering arms, and that the impious men who had conspired and fostered the rebellion were soon to experience the full penalty of their treachery, animated the breasts of our gallant fellows, and they marched on, with merry songs and light hearts, to the fatal fields in front of the Confederate capital.

But many of the poor fellows suffered sadly. Weary and foot-sore they struggle on, not a murmer passing their lips.

On the morning of May 13 we resumed our weary march about half past four o'clock. Noon came, and by that time the sun shone so hot, and the roads were so dusty, that one by one the gallant fellows dropped behind, falling from sheer exhaustion by the roadside, throwing knapsack, blankets, and other articles of the soldier's kit, recklessly away.

The scenery in that part of the country was surprisingly beautiful; but, tired out as our fellows were, they had no eye for scenic beauties. At last, completely worn out, we halted on the night of the 14th at Columbia Landing, but had orders to hold ourselves ready to march at a moment's notice. Next day it rained heavily, but marching orders did not come, for which all of us were devoutly thankful. After remaining here about twenty-four hours, we resumed our march over a road deep with mud, so deep that the wagon trains could not be moved without extra assistance. After marching about six miles, the regiment reached "White House," an estate belonging to General Lee. Here we encamped, and, having no tents with us, were again obliged to sleep in the open air. Shortly afterwards we shifted our camp to take up our proper position in line.

We remained at White House for a short time, and then proceeded to Tunstall's Station, leaving two companies behind performing "fatigue duty." These companies joined the regiment on the 20th, having been relieved. We were now within eighteen miles of Richmond, and the next day we moved four miles forward. Contrabands here swarmed about in all directions, and camps were being organized in which to keep them. There are many fine houses in that part of Virginia, and the land generally appeared to be in a good state of cultivation.

We had now arrived in Hanover County. About one o'clock, on the afternoon of the 22d of May, we again started, and, after marching about five miles, encamped in a fine field, completely surrounded by dense woods, forming a beautiful camp, having plenty of sun and shade, and good water easy of access. Heavy firing was heard the whole of the next day, and from our camp we could plainly see the balloon used by our commander in reconnoitring the position of the enemy; and being so close, we had strict orders to keep all music quiet. Our drums, therefore, were obliged to be still. We were now about ten miles and a half from Richmond.

On Saturday morning, May 24, a regiment of our brigade was ordered out on a reconnoissance. They cautiously advanced, until their skirmishers saw signs of the enemy. The regiment then dashed forward, and came upon a whole brigade of rebels. A sharp contest ensued; and, having been taken unawares, the enemy were compelled to retreat. In this skirmish, our side lost twelve killed and six wounded; they were all brought safely in, and the dead buried next day with military honors. On the following day our regiment received orders to march forward towards Richmond. They halted at a place called Gaines' Mills, within eight miles of the Confederate capital.

On the morning of Tuesday, May 27, the Ninth Regiment moved from camp, near Gaines' Mills, in light marching order. The rain poured down incessantly all the morning, which made the roads very muddy. About noon, however, the rain ceased, and the sun shone very warmly. By a circuitous route, after marching about eighteen miles, and very weary, we reached the vicinity of Hanover Court House, where a fierce fight seemed to be raging, the regiments already arrived there hailing the approach of our Bonnie Green Flag with vociferous cheering. Our boys, tired though they were, moved steadily forward, and took up their position in front. About three o'clock, the Ninth was engaged with the enemy. After several volleys, which appeared to take effect, we had orders to charge down upon a dense wood, on which the left of the rebel line rested, their whole force being under the command of General Branch. With vigorous cheers our regiment obeyed, and the long, unwavering line of the Ninth swept down upon the wood. A fierce hand-to-hand conflict ensued, in which Irish valor proved itself victorious; the enemy turned about and fled from the wood, followed by our determined lads, who pursued them to an adjoining wheat field, shooting and bayoneting them with fearful rapidity, and making prisoners of such as would yield. We captured a stand of rebel colors, and retook two guns of Martin's Battery, which had been captured by the enemy. That night the enemy, having been compelled to retire, our regiment encamped on the field, and were soon buried in sleep. In this brief contest we lost one man killed (Sergeant Regan), and eleven were wounded. We buried Regan on the field, with military honors. In passing through the woods the following day, piles of dead rebels could be seen — some bayoneted, more shot; knapsacks, blankets, and clothing of all kinds lay strewn around. In one heap we counted thirty dead men, and single forms were scattered promiscuously around, while horses were stretched in every attitude of death. This battle is known as that of Hanover Court House, and was our first engagement of any importance after the evacuation of Yorktown, on the peninsula.

On the 29th, the right wing (five companies) of our regiment was ordered on picket duty, and was relieved on the 30th. Our men were very much exhausted, having, for the last two days, eaten but two meals of coffee and army bread, commonly known as "hard tack."

CHAPTER XI.

Our Captain and the General. — Mechanicsville. — Battle of Gaines' Mill. — Battle of the Chickahominy. — Our Position after the Battle. — Night Scenes.

AFTER the stirring events mentioned in the preceding chapter, our regiment returned to Gaines' Mills, where they performed the varied duties incidental to camp life, and had an opportunity to recruit themselves after the severe ordeal their physical powers had undergone, taking their share of picket duty with other regiments.

On one occasion a detachment of one hundred men of ours, under the command of Captain John Carey, were posted at and around Newmarket Bridge, adjacent to Gaines' Mills, with special instructions to hold the bridge against the enemy at all hazards. From secret information he had received, General Fitz-John Porter was led to expect that an attack would be made on the bridge on this particular night, and feeling anxious, and knowing the importance of the position, went himself and conferred with the captain in command of the picket, "Carey of ours," as before stated. After giving minute instructions, as he was leaving, General Porter said to Carey, "Well, captain, you know what you have to do; mind, I hold you responsible;" to which the gallant captain, with his usual bluntness, replied, "Make yourself perfectly easy on that score, general; whoever passes over here must pass over the dead bodies of a hundred Irishmen." This reply may, by some, be taken as speaking boastingly; yet we can vouch for its accuracy, as expressing the confidence existing between our officers and men.

In this way the month of May and part of June were passed; nothing of importance occurring to call for remark. On the afternoon of the 26th of June the regiment marched for Mechanicsville, and, on arriving there, formed in line of battle, and took part in the engagement which took place there. We remained under fire, until the enemy was repulsed, the regiment stacking arms and sleeping on the scene of the encounter, and early in the morning we marched back to our old camp at Gaines' Mills.

Immediately on our return to camp, we received orders to cook some food, and be ready to march in half an hour, at the expiration of which time our regiment fell back about two miles, and stacked arms, prior to sending out two companies as skirmishers. Shortly afterwards we retraced our way back towards Gaines' Mills. When we arrived at the Mill Creek we found a section of Titball's United States Battery, unsupported, and gallantly contesting the passage of the bridge at the mill. The two flank companies of our regiment were then deployed as skirmishers, and shortly afterwards it was found necessary to send out two more, and finally two more companies, to support the whole.* At this time the enemy came around us so closely that they gradually overlapped our lines; we then saw that only one of two alternatives presented itself — the capture of our entire regiment or retreat. The latter, as it would still preserve to us the advantage of position, was adopted, though not until we received orders from General Griffin. We then made our retreat, gradually and slowly, contending every inch of ground, till we reached Porter's

---

* This line was gallantly commanded by Major P. T. Hanley, afterwards promoted Lieutenant Colonel.

main line. This affair was fought with indomitable firmness. When we had orders to advance and hold the Mill Creek, two other regiments had been ordered to advance with us. These regiments, however, by some misapprehension of orders, did not move forward with us. This alone would have been sufficient to intimidate most men; with the Ninth it had a contrary effect. They advanced and firmly held the position, fighting a vastly superior force, and keeping them at bay, until General Griffin gave orders to fall back; then, for the first time, the general learned that the other regiments, supposed to be coöperating with us, had not arrived on the ground, and was, therefore, greatly surprised. In this engagement we had six men killed, twenty wounded, and one missing. Proudly we write of the determination and coolness displayed by our little band in their isolated position, as only brave men can and will do. They fought, and won for themselves a name which time will hallow and preserve.

Having gradually retreated and reached the lines of General Porter, the enemy could be observed cautiously following our green flag in its retrograde movement, and then were gradually led on towards that section of the wood where our regiment had taken up its position, a fierce conflict at the same time raging over the extensive area which surrounded us. Having got our regiment into good form under the crest of a hill, we perceived, to our astonishment, that our entire army had disappeared from view, and that we, alone and unsupported, were left to meet the advancing foe; while, to add to our dismay, whole batteries, which we had lately seen in full play, and doing, as we hoped, effective service, were deserted by our men, and in full possession of the advancing hordes. An effort was being made to collect the scattered and disconnected portions of our corps in a valley about half a mile in the rear. Midway between that valley and the advancing yelling enemy, the remnant of the Ninth stood in line, amid the chaotic dispersion that reigned around. Colonels might be seen vainly striving to collect the remnants of their regiments; colors without escort; men rushing madly about, seemingly without knowing where to go, or what to do; and disaster, black and overwhelming, seeming to envelop all. Our little band, standing among the dead, hoping, longing for support, — though none came, as no troops could be rallied to that position amid the terror and confusion that prevailed, — was compelled to be the spectators of this terrible scene. Many noble fellows shed tears of anguish and rage as they looked upon the solitary flags wandering over the field in the hands of their faithful bearers, who anxiously called aloud for defenders; yet still our regiment retained its position, their colors, torn with shot and shell, still gayly fluttering in the breeze, the stars and sunburst gleaming out a calm defiance. Suddenly a rebel brigade detached itself from line, and ran forward against the position occupied by the "Ninth;" on they came, and delivered a tremendous volley, their discordant yells grating harshly upon our ears. Our regiment stood firm as statues, vigorously clutching their weapons, waiting the order of their commander. To stand was impossible; two more such volleys, and the Ninth would have been a regiment of dead! We must either go forward or retreat. It was resolved to advance. The glory that was offered was too tempting for an Irishman to resist.

Lieutenant-Colonel Guiney, who was then in command (Colonel Cass, who had been gallantly fighting all day, and who was unfit for the saddle from exhaustion, having turned over the command to his lieutenant-colonel), immediately ordered the color-bearers forward, and gave the command, "Men, follow your colors!"* Upon this our brave little line dashed forward, and delivered a galling and destructive fire, and then, coming to the charge, immediately dashed upon the enemy's lines, broke, chased, and routed them; and again, when we succeeded in driving the enemy, we hotly pressed upon his heels into an open field. This success, however, was but temporary; for the enemy, by a fierce, enfilading fire, caused our poor fellows to fall so fast, that it was deemed expedient to retire.

---

* "The Ninth Massachusetts Regiment was the rear of the retreating column which had just passed over a hill into a large, open plain. . . .

"To break and run was not for the men who had covered themselves with glory during the entire day. Colonel P. R. Guiney (now in command) decided to form a line of battle on his colors, and resist the approach of the enemy until the advance of the retreat should have been far enough to leave ground sufficient to enable him to commence his retreat in good order. Colonel Guiney, with his standard-bearers, advanced upon the rebels with the words, 'Men, follow your colors!' It was enough. Before that small band of jaded heroes waved the 'Stars and Stripes' and the 'Green Flag of Erin,' and, with loud huzzas, they rushed upon the rebels, driving them up the hill. Nine times did the remnant of the Ninth drive, with ball and buckshot, the advance of the rebel army before they could make good their retreat, the rebels being often within sixty yards of them."— *Military Correspondence of the New York Herald.*

The firing was continued without intermission, and our regiment was again forced to fall back; yet again and again they rallied, and once more dashed forward like giants, and closed with their opponents in a desperate struggle, at the same time cheering, as only Irishmen can cheer, their idolized emblem still at their front, waving its folds amid the torrent of bullets and clouds of smoke which enveloped it, and driving the enemy back, step by step, they regained more ground than they had lost.

But our gallant regiment, decimated by the shot and shell of the enemy, exhausted by the rapid fighting of eight consecutive hours, without food, many of them falling from thirst and exhaustion, paused in their victorious career, vainly striving to advance against the overwhelming legions of the enemy. But all their valor was in vain. They fell back, step by step, sending to their foes the leaden messengers of defiance. Human nature could do no more; but at last, in the sullen savageness of despair, with heroic determination, they rallied again, and rushed once more on the astonished foe; again they fell back; these terrific encounters were repeated nine times in succession. General officers, separated from their commands, fired with enthusiasm by the gallant conduct of our men, joined with them in these fearful conflicts. Thus the fierce struggle went on with alternate success until darkness came on, and the enemy withdrew from the contest.

Dusk was fast approaching, and our men, weary and worn out, taking advantage of the lull which ensued, threw themselves carelessly down upon the hill-side, striving to forget in sleep the gloom and disaster of the day. Gloomy, indeed, it was; the dead and the living intermingled, while, occasionally, a moan or cry of anguish from some poor, maimed, bruised, or dying soldier, as he strove to ease the pain of his gaping wounds, begged for water to moisten his parched tongue, or cool his throbbing brow; again the frenzied cry of a sufferer, the intensity of whose pain had hurled lordly reason from its throne, — all these would rouse the tired soldier, though but for a moment, and again he slept on, strange though it may seem. Meanwhile, the night progressed slowly, its monotony only broken by the deep breathing of the sleeping men of our regiment, or the agonized cry of the wounded around us — then followed by an oppressing silence. The night had far advanced, when, looking toward the valley before mentioned, we discerned what seemed to be compact masses of troops approaching; nearer and nearer they came, until they reached the hill whereon we lay; then, in the feeble light, we gladly hailed the "green and gold" banner of "Meagher's Immortal Brigade." They had come to relieve us. They greeted us with rousing cheers which we as heartily returned, and resigned to them the position we had held during the day.*

In a report of this battle by "A Prussian Officer," the credit of the action has been given to the "Irish Brigade;" on the contrary, they took no part in the battle of the Chickahominy; it was the green flag of the Ninth that deceived the "Prussian Officer," and occasioned the statement in his report.

The glory of that day cost us too much blood to be easily parted with.†

---

* "The Ninth Regiment (Massachusetts Volunteers), with a handful of regulars, were the last to leave the field." — *General Marcy.* (Vide Slocum's Report.)

† "The billows of battle raged fiercely around. The struggle was man to man, eye to eye, and bayonet to bayonet. The hostile 'Meagher Brigade' [the Ninth Massachusetts Volunteers], com-

From the general officers of our division, our regiment received expressions of satisfaction and admiration for their courageous and heroic de-

posed chiefly of Irishmen, offered heroic resistance. After a fierce struggle our people were compelled to give way, and at length all orders and encouragements were in vain. They were falling back in great disorder. Infuriate, foaming at the mouth, bareheaded, sabre in hand, at this critical moment General Cobb appeared upon the field at the head of his legion, and with him the Nineteenth North Carolina and Fourteenth Virginia.

"At once the troops renewed the attack, but all their devotion and sacrifice were in vain. The Irish held their position with a determination and ferocity that called forth the admiration of our own officers. Broken to pieces and disorganized, the fragments of that fine legion came rolling back from the charge. The Ninteenth North Carolina lost eight standard-bearers, and most of their staff-officers were either killed or wounded. Again Generals Hill and Andrews led their troops to the attack, and some regiments covered themselves with immortal glory. Our troops exhibited a contempt of death that made them the equal of old, experienced veterans; for, notwithstanding the bloody harvest the destroyer reaped in our ranks that day, no disorder, no timid bearing, revealed that many of the regiments were under fire for the first time. But the enemy, nevertheless, quietly and coolly held out against every attack we made, one after the other, notwithstanding the fact that this solitary brigade had to stand their ground from four until eight o'clock P. M. They [the Ninth] performed feats of incredible valor; and it was only when the news came that Jackson was upon them in the rear, at about eight, they retired before our advance. Despite the dreadful carnage in their ranks, they marched on with streaming banners and rolling drums, and carried with them all their slightly wounded and all their baggage, and, when the cavalry of Davis and Wickham went in pursuit, repelled this assault with perfect coolness." — *The Peninsular Campaign. By a Prussian Officer* (Rebel).

fence of a most exposed position, for many hours, against a vastly superior force. In the closer phases of the conflict the desperate strength of the Irish soldier made tremendous havoc among the ranks of the enemy. On that day the Ninth won great renown, and by their bravery showed themselves worthy of the land which gave them birth and of maintaining the honor of their adopted country.

In this action we lost Captains Madigan, Carey, O'Neil, and McCafferty, and Lieutenants Frank O'Dowd and Richard P. Nugent, who fell gallantly fighting while discharging their duties. Our total loss in this engagement was seventy-one killed, one hundred and thirty wounded, and fifteen missing.

CHAPTER XII.

Malvern Hill. — The Battle. — Gallant Charges. — Death of Colonel Cass. — He is succeeded by Colonel Guiney. — Harrison's Landing. — A Scare. — Straps and no Straps. — A Night's Rest disturbed.

ON the morning following the battle of the Chickahominy, we recrossed the river in fine order, and bivouacked upon its banks, where we remained until the following day, when we marched to Malvern Hill. The men of the Ninth were in good spirits, having the fullest confidence in General McClellan, and moved forward with the warmest anticipations of success. We arrived at Malvern Hill in the afternoon, and immediately took up a position on the heights, which we occupied until midnight. After changing our position several times, we were sent as a support to the artillery which was in position on the plain running from the base of Malvern Hill. Here our forces were much exposed, no natural advantage of ground intervening between ourselves and the enemy, who were posted in line of battle in a dense wood, which formed a semicircle around the position held by the Union troops. Our principal strength consisted in the immense guns planted in our rear, which shelled the woods unceasingly, and in our fleet of gunboats, which, though some two miles distant, rendered efficient service, and caused some terrible destruction. About nine o'clock the artillery of the contending forces opened fire, and continued it with great vigor for nearly three hours, terrible execution being done on both sides.

About one o'clock the columns of the enemy, under General Magruder, advanced boldly and rapidly from the wood, with the intention of seizing the batteries in position on the plain. A terrific storm of grape-shot greeted them as they came on. Again and again the cannons blazed forth their murderous rage, and whole ranks fell down, actually shattered and blown to pieces; yet still the brave fellows came on, closer and closer to the batteries, until they seemed in imminent danger of being taken, when General Griffin, who had command of the artillery, exclaimed, "*Up and at them, Ninth!*"

The words had scarcely passed his lips when Colonel Cass, turning to his gallant fellows, gave the command, " Charge !" Our men then sprang forward to the front of the cannon, and dashed on the advancing foe. The enemy paused for an instant ; their line wavered ; a moment more it broke, and fled to the woods. Here Colonel Cass fell mortally wounded. The artillery of the enemy now opened fire upon the regiment, compelling us to retire. The conflict that followed that glorious charge baffles description. It was a series of brilliant charges on both sides. The tenacity of the combatants in their fierce struggle for the victory, and the desperate ferocity which animated them, are scarcely paralleled in the history of battles. Colonel Thomas Cass was brought safely from the field. He was very badly wounded, but the surgeon who attended him when he was carried to the rear expressed hopes of his recovery. In this, we are grieved to say, he was mistaken. He was taken home to Boston, where he expired July 12, 1862. He was an able soldier. He served his country well, and will ever hold a distinguished place in her history.

Lieutenants John H. Rafferty and Edward McSweeny were killed in this engagement. They fell fighting bravely at the head of their companies. Young, brave, and generous, their loss was deeply felt.

The battle closed at nightfall. At midnight, General McClellan had evacuated his position, and the following morning the bulk of his army was at Harrison's Landing, on the banks of the James River, where the Ninth Regiment encamped until August 14, 1862. It was at Harrison's Landing that the Ninth — in fact, the whole army of the Potomac — learned, for the first time, that they had been defeated, and that the campaign upon the peninsula was a failure.

Colonel P. R. Guiney, who succeeded Colonel Cass in the command of the Ninth Regiment, was born in Ireland, at Parkstown, in the County of Tipperary, having come to this country when a boy of eight years. He was educated to the profession of law, and admitted to practice in 1856. Upon the breaking out of the rebellion, he threw aside his legal pursuits, and took an active part in the organization of the Ninth Regiment, and came with it into the field with the rank of captain. For " meritorious and gallant conduct at the battle of the Chickahominy"* he was raised, upon the death of Colonel Cass, to the colonelcy of the Ninth Regiment, by a special order of General Fitz-John Porter who commanded the corps upon the peninsula, which special order was published in all the papers of Massachusetts after its receipt at the State House, by order of His Excellency, Governor John A. Andrew, and was really the only public acknowledgment made of the services of the regiment that had done so much. Colonel Guiney assumed command of the Ninth Regiment at Harrison's Landing in August, 1862.

The country in the vicinity of Harrison's Landing has been aptly termed the "Eden of Virginia;" but, when the army of McClellan gathered itself together the morning after the terrible battle of Malvern Hill, and moved towards the landing, the ripening fields of wheat and corn, in all their golden luxuriance, were trampled under foot, and the beautiful picture of plenty and peace passed like a *mirage* from the view; and before the night of that day the scene that presented itself defies description. It

---

* See Report of the Adjutant-General of Massachusetts for 1862, p. 30.

was a desolate sight to behold the remnant of that once splendid army of the Potomac huddled together under the pelting storm, without shelter, without food, knee-deep in mud, weary and exhausted, vainly seeking a dry spot whereon to stretch their sore and tired limbs.

In spite of the great discomforts of that day, one could scarce forbear smiling as he beheld the soldiers plodding their way through the mud. A step, and down they would go, leaving shoes and boots behind them with placid resignation, knowing that it was useless to struggle, and finally sinking from sheer exhaustion. Millions worth of property was destroyed upon the route. In the fields, wagons and commissary stores of all kinds were piled together and burned to prevent them from falling into the hands of the enemy. Barrels of sugar, coffee, pork, rice, beans, and boxes of bread, were recklessly flung into the roads, or piled in masses and set fire to. Public and private stores shared the same fate. The luxuries of the general were flung into the same blaze that consumed the coarse necessaries of the soldier. No distinctions were made; destruction was the order of the day; and everything that could not be transported was given over to the destroying element.

When the soldiers witnessed this dire destruction, they could no longer doubt the magnitude of their misfortune. Those burning piles were significant of defeat, and they turned their eyes, sad and dispirited, in the direction of the Landing, where were gathered the transports that were soon, they supposed, to take them from the scenes of their great disasters.

The rebel army were, however, in a far worse condition than ourselves. They were actually starving, and, fortunately for us, in the language of the Prussian officer, Colonel Estvan, "they had no army with which to pursue us." *

Officers of every grade were down at the Landing, having no commands, and waiting for an opportunity to get aboard the transports. One of these, General F——, was engaged in a controversy with one of our men, Peter McQueeny, a quaint fellow, of infinite humor. The general had ordered Peter to do something, which the latter refused, on the ground that the general had no command over him, and had no straps upon his shoulder to indicate his rank.

"I'm General F——, fellow," cried that dignitary.

---

* See Report of Peninsular Campaign. By a Prussian Officer.

"Excuse me, gineral," said Peter, with a droll salute; "I thought you was some other loafer!"

The crowd laughed heartily, and the disconcerted general very soon disappeared.

One night, about twelve o'clock, when we were all buried in slumber, a rebel battery was run down to the bank upon the other side of the river, and opened fire upon us. The shells went shrieking through the air, dropping in every direction; men, roused from their slumbers, ran wildly about, ducking their heads in the most comical manner, in vain search for a place of security.

Indeed, they had good cause for the fear they manifested; for the shell exploded all around them, creating immense confusion and doing considerable damage. What made the matter worse was the fact that we were utterly helpless, and had to stand the brunt of the enemy's fire without the power to return it.

The shells were flying among the shipping, and sailors and soldiers jumped into the river, where they were in more danger of getting hit, and struck out for shore, where, when they had arrived, they found the missiles more plentiful and destructive than on shipboard.

The excitement lasted for nearly an hour, when the aerial demons ceased to fly, much to the satisfaction of our men, who muttered tender blessings on the heads of those that caused the mischief.

Strange to say, none were injured in our regiment, though one man was struck dead in the Sixty-second Pennsylvania Regiment, which was encamped next to us.

CHAPTER XIII.

We leave Harrison's Landing. — Visit Miner's Hill. — Sad Recollec tions. — McClellan again resumes Command. — Invasion of Mary land. — Battle of Antietam. — Retreat of Lee.

THE Ninth remained at Harrison's Landing till August 14, 1862; thence they marched down the peninsula, *en route* for Fortress Monroe, passing, on their way, through nearly all our old camps. Again we beheld the result of our labors in front of Yorktown. With what different emotions we gazed upon them! Our memories naturally reverted to the gallant dead who had cheerfully labored with us in those intrenchments, and who now sleep forever on the bloody field of the Chickahominy, or the plains of Malvern. We had started from this place with exultant hearts — the enemy in flight before us; we returned drooping and dispirited — a triumphant enemy behind us. But we had our scars and our glory; and our virgin flags had been baptized in the fierce fire of five battles, and we had even wrested victory from ruinous defeat.

Our march was rapidly continued, and in about five days we reached Fortress Monroe, where we remained for a short time, receiving there a number of recruits from Massachusetts, who were enthusiastically welcomed. Thence we marched to Newport News, where we embarked for Acquia Creek, which we reached the next day. From that place we went by rail to Fredericksburg, encamping at Stafford Heights, where we remained two or three days. From this camp we marched, on the 24th of August, to Ellis' Ford, on the Rappahannock, where we watched and waited for about a week, and then proceeded to Warrenton Junction. Leaving that place we went on to Manassas, and participated in all the disastrous encounters which occurred there. Our regiment, however, did not suffer, as we only had five wounded. We then proceeded, via Vienna, to Chain Bridge, on the Potomac, whence we returned to our old camp at Miner's Hill, after an absence of nearly six months. We marched slowly and silently up the hill, familiar scenes meeting us on every hand; we passed over the pathways which had been worn by the feet of the men of the Ninth; we reached the old parade ground, where we had so often stood in the pride of full ranks; sadly and silently we marched into the company streets; the tall weeds nearly obscured the cellars we had dug the last winter; the old seats and shelves we had erected still remained.

The ashes of the old camp fires were still visible, and the tent poles we had stuck into the ground still remained standing. One by one our poor fellows pitched their tents. In a little while all was done; then the history of the last few months became painfully evident. The vacant cellars could be seen on every hand. The men who had once lived, laughed, and sung within them were dead. The officers' tents were pitched in line. Another terrible *hiatus* appeared. Company I's tent was not pitched; its cellar was not covered; its officers had not returned. All had been killed on the peninsula.

In a few days the broken corps of the army of the Potomac were gathered before the works that protected Washington, and the process of reorganization was commenced by General McClellan, who had again assumed control of the army, after the disastrous campaign of Pope.

About this time rumors were rife that General Lee meditated the invasion of Maryland. Soon corps after corps moved on Washington.

On the 12th of September our regiment started, and, recrossing the Potomac at Georgetown, reached the capital, which was in a state of great excitement.

The threatened invasion of the northern states, and the dire rumors that the capital itself was menaced, was sufficient material for the most intense feeling, and the progress of the army of the Potomac was watched with anxiety; the citizens greeted them with great demonstrations of affection and delight. In their compact ranks and brown faces they showed little of the wreck of the peninsula, and the recruits since received greatly enlarged their columns. Two days' rapid marching, under a hot sun, and over dusty roads, brought us to Leesburg, in Maryland. The following day we passed through Rockville and Clarksburg, halting on the night of the 13th, near Hyattstown — a most insignificant place, with scarcely provision enough to feed a chicken. A place called Urbana is another effort of mind over matter, but is somewhat dignified by its vicinity to Monocacy Station. We staid here a few hours, and then resumed our march, arriving at Frederick City, in Maryland. In these four days the Ninth marched nearly one hundred miles, — in the best possible humor, and every day in anticipation of an engagement. The regiment passed immediately through Frederick, by way of Middleton, and, on the morning of the 17th of September, the Ninth joined in the well-fought field of Antietam, our regiment being employed in supporting Griffin's United States Battery D. The progress of this engagement was remarkably splendid; the masses of our army were moved with precision and celerity, our charging columns moving forward unwaveringly; and the entire army moved under the influence of one will, carrying fear and consternation into the ranks of the enemy, the determined and valorous fighting of the northern soldiers being terribly conspicuous; and terror reigned in all the ranks of the rebel horde. McClellan vigorously assailed the retreating forces of the enemy, driving them to the Potomac, where they would have been almost annihilated but for the extraordinary lowness of the water in the river, and the unfortunate surrender of the Loudon Heights, and the works and defences about Harper's Ferry.

CHAPTER XIV.

Scenes at Antietam and South Mountain. — The doomed Legion. — Insults offered to Union Soldiers. — Hospital Scenes. — Yankee Smartness. — Be careful of your Stars. — It is finished. — A miscreant Regiment. — Boteler's Mills. — Picket Duty. — End of First Maryland Campaign.

THE battle-fields of South Mountain and Antietam showed a frightful loss of human life. The dead were thickly strewn about the roads and piled in stagnant ditches, in some cases hidden by the cornstalks and grass, in many instances frightfully mutilated by the feet of the immense bodies of cavalry and infantry that had passed over them in the progress of the terrific struggle. As we slowly and carefully picked our way along, long lines of the soiled gray coats of the dead enemy showed the position in which they had been placed, and which they were instructed to maintain at all hazards, and in defending which they had perished gallantly. Blue coats and gray coats were lying side by side, their quarrels over; though in " life divided, yet in death united." Wounded men were thickly scattered around, and many of them had lain for two nights upon the field before they were removed to the hospital. Upon some of the bodies of the dead rebels we noticed papers attached, giving the name of the unfortunate men, and requesting that their graves might be marked, as a means of future identification. One of the most revolting scenes we have ever witnessed actually came under our notice. This was after the engagement of South Mountain, two days before the decisive battle of Antietam. We came to a field enclosed on every side by stone walls, literally covered with dead men, in indescribable confusion. These were the remains of the Georgia Legion, under the command of General Howell Cobb. They had marched into the enclosure, there to hold the position at the base of the mountain; they were then instantly attacked by our troops on all sides, and literally destroyed. Cavalry, infantry, and artillery simultaneously assailed them, and scarce one man of that fine legion escaped to tell the story of its fate! There they lay in all attitudes of death; some stiff and cold, in the act of firing; some calmly lay, as if in sleep; others appeared like living men resting against trees which were there; again there were masses of dead, many maimed, bruised, and so mangled by shot and shell as scarcely to retain the appearance of human beings. It was a terrible picture of human ferocity, and yet scarcely expressed a tittle of the horrors of that campaign.

Houses and barns in the vicinity of the battle-fields were used for hospital purposes, and these were filled with wounded men, mostly rebels. Low platforms were raised before the doors of many of these houses, on which would be stretched the figure of a man, one of whose limbs would be in process of amputation. Rebel surgeons worked side by side with Union surgeons, and, unlike doctors in general, seemed to agree most cordially. Amputated arms and legs were flung unconcernedly upon the ground, and sometimes carelessly handled and examined by the soldiers whose curiosity led them to be spectators of the scene.

Ladies, richly dressed, would come from the adjacent places to visit the rebel wounded, bringing with them jellies, wines, and preserved meats, which they would give to our wounded prisoners, passing the poor northern soldier upon his bed of racking pain, without a word or look of sympathy, or a drop of the precious liquid with which they cooled the lips of the wounded traitor. Many of the rebels expressed hopes that the war would soon be over, and more of them spoke of the North with great bitterness, and said that only by a war of extermination would the South be beaten; many of them asserted the superiority of their soldiers over ours, which we thought displayed considerable hardihood, after the terrible whipping we had just given them; but it was made seemingly with full reliance in its truth. The wounded men left in our hands by the rebels amounted to several thousands, a number of whom were conscripts. These received every care from our surgeons and their own, as well as from visitors; and our lads, with noble generosity, supplied them with such necessaries as they could command, in the shape of tobacco, pipes, &c., for which they seemed very thankful. They were eager to exchange their "scrip" for our greenbacks, sometimes offering ten dollars in scrip for one dollar in our currency.

Owing to the care taken, very few of those injured died, and as soon as they recovered were sent to Washington, and shortly after their arrival would be exchanged.

Scenes like these could be witnessed about Sharpsburg, and within less than half a mile of the Potomac, and in the immediate vicinity of the camp occupied by the Ninth. Our men paid daily visits to the hospitals containing the rebel wounded, and many of them contracted friendships which they afterwards found very useful, some when wounded on the battle-field, and others when in the prisons at Richmond.

We remember an incident which occurred one day before one of these temporary hospitals. A rebel surgeon was busily engaged in amputating the leg of one of his own men, and at the same time conversing with a tall, muscular man, of the "Maine lumber" species. In the course of his work the surgeon laid down a small pair of scissors, which the tall Yankee picked up, and seemed to examine with great curiosity, at the same time turning his eyes upon one of the glittering stars adorning the collar of the doctor's coat, indicating his rank in the rebel service. By a dexterous, and, to us, almost imperceptible application of the scissors, the Yankee filched one of the stars, and, whistling the national air, walked coolly away.

In a short time the doctor noticed the loss of

his star; he looked about for his Yankee friend; not seeing him, at last he said, "Well, gentlemen, I've never been *north,* but I've heard a great deal about Yankee *smartness,* and wooden hams and nutmegs, and I concluded the 'Yanks' were pretty smart; but I never *did* think one of them smart enough to steal a star from under a man's chin before!" Another, though painful incident, occurred here. A boy, about fourteen years old, was one day undergoing the process of amputation. He lay upon the stage, dressed in his rebel uniform, his face pale, and his large blue eyes gazing wonderingly around. His injured leg was stretched before the surgeons, who were carefully feeling it about the wound — a black break, about the size of a nickel cent. A sign from one of the doctors, and the instruments were brought and placed upon a large box that once contained army clothes, but now was partly filled with bandages besmeared with blood. The surgeon selected one of the instruments; a cloth was held before the nostrils of the white-faced boy; the surgeon began his work. The skin of the white leg was cut; in a little while the bone was off, the arteries taken up, the skin laid over, the bandages applied, and the whole bound carefully up. "It is finished," said the doctor, as he wiped the blood from off his hands. He said truly; the work was finished. *The boy was dead!*

On the evening of the 18th of September, while lying close to the banks of the Potomac, we received orders to move. The enemy were reported to be in force on the other side of the river, and a sharp fight was anticipated. The One Hundred and Eighteenth Pennsylvania Volunteers were ordered to cross the river and engage the enemy posted on the high bluffs overlooking the Potomac. The river, or that part of it which divided us from the enemy, was scarcely two hundred yards wide, and easily fordable. The One Hundred and Eighteenth immediately took to the water, and moved across the river. As they approached the opposite bank, the enemy opened a fierce fire upon them. The Pennsylvanians halted, staggered a moment, and then, seized with panic, turned about and fled. But this desertion of the flag was fiercely avenged; for our batteries upon the bank hurled their shot and shrapnel among them until they attacked the enemy, who captured a large number of them. But the true metal of the Fourth Michigan, backed by the Irish Ninth, turned the fate of the battle, and in a short time, after a fierce and gallant contest, the enemy retreated, leaving in our hands a number of prisoners and several pieces of artillery.

This engagement is known as that of Boteler's Mills. It is the same place where General Banks destroyed so many millions worth of rebel property, including all the mills in that vicinity from which the rebels were supplied with grain, upon his famous retreat from the Shenandoah. In this engagement two pieces of the artillery captured were found to be of those which were taken by the enemy at the first battle of Bull Run. General Griffin was exceedingly pleased at this recapture, and highly complimented the gallantry of his brigade. One of the guns taken here turned out to have been one of those taken from the general's battery at the first battle of Bull Run.

Next day our regiment encamped a few yards from the banks of the Potomac, having its picket posted close to the river, as it was deemed unadvisable to post a force on the other side. In a few days the enemy's picket gradually advanced, and moved down to the banks of the river, on the opposite side, and opened communication with our lads, and in a little while a very good feeling seemed to prevail between them. Our men would bathe in their own side of the river, and hold interesting conversations at the same time with a rebel on the other side, who, leaning on his gun, would watch our lads as they disported themselves in the water. Papers would be exchanged, and tobacco and coffee; and, in fact, a proper "picket feeling" was soon established.

On arriving at the bank of the Potomac, the Maryland campaign was virtually ended. It was a rapid and glorious one for General McClellan and his army, and caused much rejoicing in the Northern States.

At its conclusion, unlike that of the peninsular campaign, our army was in splendid condition, and ready for an immediate move. It is not in our power, even if we had the desire, to state the reason of the idle days which ensued, but we have the fullest confidence in General McClellan, and feel sure that he had good reasons for that delay, and have no doubt the history of the rebellion will fully justify them.

CHAPTER XV.

Crossing the Potomac under Difficulties. — Shepherdstown. — Rebel Chaff. — That was all it was fit for. — A neat Thing in Shawls. — We find the Enemy. — Return to Camp. — Sharpsburg.

ONE morning our cavalry crossed the river, causing the enemy's picket to fall hastily back; our troopers followed them rapidly, felt the enemy after a ride of nearly twenty miles, and, after a slight skirmish, returned to camp. An infantry reconnoissance was speedily projected, and, among others, our regiment ordered out. We crossed the river, finding the water in some places very deep, and through which our men had to wade, the water reaching to their waist, causing them much trouble to secure their arms and ammunition from getting wet. We crossed with but little opposition, and proceeded cautiously forward, our force being under the command of General Humphrey. After a short march, we reached Shepherdstown, where we learned that a strong force of the enemy had just passed through, their rear being but about an hour's march in advance; our line was halted, and a strong body of skirmishers deployed to feel the enemy and secure our advance.

We rested in the main street, awaiting information from the front, and had, therefore, plenty of time for observation.

Shepherdstown seemed to have been quite an enterprising place formerly, as it contained plenty of stores, but with very little in them; what there was, was marked at such exorbitant prices as to find but few purchasers. A large number of paroled rebel officers and soldiers could be seen; the former, in most cases, looking from windows, *tête à tête* with pretty female rebels, who looked with cold disdain upon our bold fellows as they rested upon the curbstones, gazing curiously about them, while the rebels sauntered round, with their hands deep in their trousers pockets, ventilating their "tatters," asking impertinent questions, and gratuitously informing us that we should leave Shepherdstown, not as we entered it, with a twenty-eight inch step, but at a gait commonly known as the "double-quick."

That very useful northern expression known

as "Gas," was the only reply deigned by our boys, who looked at their tormentors and their "tatters" with eyes of supreme contempt.

It was easy to be seen that the inhabitants of this town bore us little good will, though they were greatly astonished at the fine, comfortable appearance of our soldiers; at the full haversack and the abundance of coffee and sugar they carried, and which some exchanged for tobacco: coffee, sugar, and such necessaries, could scarcely be purchased in Shepherdstown. On one side of the street was a miserable, dilapidated-looking shanty, with the legend "TAILOR" overhead; within was a wee little old man, doing a large business; that is, putting an extremely large patch upon a very mean coat, belonging to a rebel officer sick in the town; a bench, sleeve-board, and a heavy goose, were the only "chattels and appurtenances" the place contained. That tailor's shop seemed to be the only paying establishment in the place.

As an example of the good will manifested towards us, we may relate an incident which happened there.

A female stood at one of the garden gates, with a large warm flour cake in her hands, which she held temptingly before some of the Union soldiers, as if waiting for them to purchase. If that *was* her intention, she was soon successful, for one of our men stepped up and asked her what she would take for the cake? She looked at him sourly for an instant, and then, with an insulting laugh, threw the cake to a dog that was near. The insulted soldier gazed on her for a moment with an eye of fire; but then, recollecting himself, turned away with a smile, saying, " I beg your pardon, madam; *that* was all it was fit for." Whenever any of the inhabitants could insult a Union soldier, it would be done; but our men bore their taunts and sarcasms with great good humor, rarely, if ever, replying to them. The churches and public buildings in the town had been turned into hospitals, and the yellow flags that waved from their roofs indicated that they contained quite a large number of wounded, who had been unable to leave the place on our approach, and, therefore, had been paroled. The inhabitants, however, did not scruple to make great complaints about the scarcity of provisions and the large prices demanded for what was to be had. A soldier chanced to ask a lady for a match to light his pipe (she was standing at the door), and in a moment supplied him with one, merely remarking, "You are welcome to it, sir; I would give you more, but they cost a dollar per box." Notwithstanding her politeness, she was a downright rebel, but had many lady-like qualities. The soldier presented her with some coffee, which she gratefully accepted; it was, indeed, quite a luxury. As a general thing, we found that the *old* ladies were very kind and very polite, keeping their opinions to themselves, and treating our soldiers with considerable affability. The *young* women, however, were sometimes quite ferocious; not very select in their language, or dignified in their demeanor. This was owing, perhaps, to the great scarcity of young men, who had been conscripted from their "side," or had voluntarily gone to fight the "black invaders."

But few men were to be found in the town, and those, with the exception of some on parole, as before mentioned, were aged and unserviceable; the good and healthy material had been seized upon long ago, or had volunteered, and were then in our front, or hidden in the town, until they could safely leave on our departure. We had halted in Shepherdstown about an hour, when we received orders to move forward. As we advanced, crowds of women and boys, black and white, lined the sidewalks, making remarks by no means complimentary either to our humanity or honesty. Moving on, we came in sight of a group of black women, who clapped their fat hands in seeming ecstasy as they saw our compact mass of troops approaching with glistening arms and martial bearing, forming, we have no doubt, a striking contrast to the rebel troops, who had hastily left the town before us. As our Green Flag was seen, fluttering its golden glories upon the breeze, by a passing group of colored wenches, one of them, extraordinary in rotundity and luxurious in fat, clapped her hands, exclaiming, "See dar! ain't dat beautiful!" To which a vinegar-faced white woman pointedly replied, "It is, indeed; it would make a very handsome shawl, with that fine gold border." Whether the sharp-nosed female intended a sarcasm or not, we could not tell; but it looked and sounded to us very much like it.

We marched some ten miles beyond Shepherdstown, and halted for a while, sending skirmishers out on our flanks. A rumor came down the line that our advance had overtaken the enemy, who was in position some distance ahead, and well protected by artillery. We had been halted but a few minutes when heavy firing commenced. The reconnoissance began to assume very large dimensions; in fact, it looked as if a sharp fight was in progress. Suddenly the fierce shriek of a shell, rapidly hissing through the air, attracted our attention, and, turning to see where it had struck, we beheld one man of Company H lying on the ground, a pool of blood rapidly accumulating round his head; a piece of shell had struck him on the left side of the head, behind the ear, dangerously wounding him. He was moved into an adjoining field on a stretcher, where we left him with the surgeon of our regiment. The man's name was Mullen, belonging to Milford.

After firing heavily for some time, we made another advance, and in a short time had the pleasure of driving the enemy.

Having discovered his whereabouts, the object for which we started was attained; and towards night we marched back, and after moving from place to place for nearly an hour, and throwing out pickets, and calling them in, — all this time under a pelting rain, and up to our knees in mud, — we continued our march, and, late in the night, re-crossed the Potomac, again wading through, and, weary, wet, exhausted, and thoroughly miserable, laid ourselves down by our fires to sleep and dry our clothes.

CHAPTER XVI.

A social Evening. — Presence of Mind. — A startling Narrative. — A Cure for Bores. — How it was effected.

ONE day, while at Sharpsburg, a number of us were seated around a large log fire in an adjoining camp to that of ours, and conversing on a variety of subjects. Finally one of the party related Jerrold's bit of humor on "Presence of Mind." Said he, "The subject arose in Jerrold's presence as to the value of that faculty, and some one said, 'Yes, it was very valuable, especially when attacked by a mad bull or dog.' 'Ay,' returned Jerrold, 'in that case presence of mind is very good, but absence of body is better.'" In a little while "presence of mind" became the subject matter of conversation; and one of the party, a large, fat, jolly captain, noted for telling "whopping big stories," remarked that *he* exhibited that valuable faculty in a most wonderful manner.

"How? let's hear it, captain," queried the party, with a great deal of interest. The fat captain puffed forth an immense volume of smoke, and, settling himself more comfortably on his "hard-tack" box, proceeded to unburden himself to the following effect:—

"You may know, boys, that I trapped and hunted for a considerable time in the Canadas; and a most exciting life I led, I tell you. Many a time I've camped out on the snowy hills, with nothing but a heavy coat of buffalo skin for extra covering, making myself as comfortable as I could in a log hut of my own construction, living principally on dried meats — trapping, killing foxes, and other animals I could find, and now and then capturing a bear, whose skins at that time were very valuable. Well, one morning I got up pretty early, and started out to look at my traps. I left my rifle behind me, and with my snow-shoes on, hurried as rapidly as I could over the snow-covered hills. The morning was very cold, and my muffler was closely wrapped around my head, almost covering my eyes, and obstructing my vision. I had walked about a mile, and had just reached an immense shelf of rock, forming a precipice several hundred feet deep, when I heard a deep growl, and, turning about, beheld a huge black bear within a few feet of me. I tell you, boys, I was rather astonished, and somewhat *skeered*. Before I could make up my mind what to do, the bear leaped upon me; and the first thing I knew distinctly was, that I was clinging on the edge of the rock, and hanging over the frightful precipice. Boys, I tell you it was a fearful predicament for a man of my rotundity, and I thought I was 'gone up.'"

"Gone up!" cried one of the listeners; "gone *down*, you mean."

"Hush, Sammy," quoth the captain, reprovingly; "you don't understand these things. Well, as I was saying, I thought I was gone *up*. However, I made up my mind to hang on as long as I could, when the bear, who had been looking at me, turned about and was going off. An idea struck me. With wonderful presence of mind I seized the bear by the hind leg, — he gave a howl, bounded forward, and dragged me to the top of the ledge, and left me there safe and sound! Talk of presence of mind — pshaw! show me anything to equal that!" and the fat captain puffed away more vigorously than ever, whilst a look of gentle satisfaction stole across his plump physiogomy. We listened to him with mingled admiration and interest, wishing to ask him what he and the bear did when he came so unexpectedly back to the top of the ledge; but we feared a more tremendous whopper, so deemed it prudent to remain silent. At last, one daring fellow had the temerity to put the query. "What did we do?" repeated the captain, in a slight state of bewilderment; "what did we do? Why, you don't suppose I would hurt a hair of that bear's head, do you, after saving my life? No, no; *I just let him go — I just let him go. I did!*"

We all knew that Munchausen was a minor light compared with the "fat captain;" but one of the officers of the assembled party knew this better than ourselves, and as he was one of the captain's lieutenants, he was continually bored with the tremendous yarns he used to tell; therefore he determined to put a stop to them in some way. He arranged a plan, and, strange to say, was remarkably successful.

The way of it was this. The officer who had undertaken the cure went, one day, to a hospital where the wounded rebel prisoners were, and secured a leg which had just been amputated, and had it secretly conveyed to the tent occupied by himself and the talkative captain. At night, taking advantage of the temporary absence of his fat friend, he settled himself in bed, and placed the inanimate leg by his side so as to allow the foot partly to protrude from underneath the bed-clothes. The captain soon after entered the tent, and heard his chum moaning piteously.

"What's the matter, Dick?" asked the captain.

"O, I've got an awful cramp in my left leg; it pains me fearfully; O! O!"

"I'll soon fix that for you, Dick," cried the captain. "Where's your leg?"

"Here, this one," said Dick, indicating the position of the substituted limb by a gesture, at the same time moaning, and taking the precaution to hold it firmly in a sort of natural position.

"Whew! it's awful cold, boy," exclaimed Munchausen, seizing hold of the protruding foot. "You'll freeze a fellow if he gets into that bed;" and he gave it a pull.

"How is it now, Dick?"

"Pull again," urged Dick. Another pull, and

"Presence of mind" of the Fat Captain. Page 141.

another; the sweat standing in great drops on the fat man's brow.

"How is it now, Dick?"

"O, it's awful," groaned the victim; this time the captain gave a tremendous jerk. The leg gave way, and the fat servant of Uncle Sam was flung upon his back with what he thought the severed limb of his unfortunate companion in his hands! A howl of poignant anguish, intermingled with smothered laughter, rung out upon the night air, calling every one from their beds to the tent, where they beheld the victimized captain in a state of horror and amazement, gazing upon the dead limb lying before him. He was incapable of speech or motion. He had, as he imagined, destroyed his beloved comrade, and his extremity was such that the valuable faculty, "presence of mind," which he boasted he possessed to such a remarkable degree (vide "the bear story" and others equally demonstrative), had entirely deserted him; but the roars of Dick, and the uncontrollable laughter of the crowd, brought him soon to his senses. He looked around, saw Dick sitting on the bed, boasting the ownership of two good legs. A light broke in upon him; he jumped up with a look of disgust, and, with many anathemas, went to his chest, opened it, placed the decanters upon the table, lit his pipe, and was soon enveloped in a cloud of smoke.

The cure was an effective one, and we never afterwards heard the captain (though we met him several times) indulge in detailing his extraordinary personal reminiscences.

Another specimen of humor was perpetrated at this camp upon a regimental surgeon, nearly as good as the former. A certain officer, desirous of tasting the doctor's brandy, which, by the by, was rarely produced, went to him one morning and said, —

"Doctor, an old ailing of mine has returned after an absence of about a year, and I fear, if not soon attended to, the consequences will be serious; as it is, it totally unfits me for duty."

"What is it, lieutenant?" asked the doctor, blandly, as he motioned the patient to a seat.

"I don't know exactly what to term it, doctor," replied our friend. "My arm is completely dead, and I find it utterly impossible to move it;" and, with a very doleful expression, he lifted up the "*deceased*" limb, holding it with the right hand under the scrutiny of the doctor. The officer wore one of the heavy military coats with wide sleeves, which he kept closed together with his hand. The doctor took hold of the arm, and started with astonishment when he felt how cold it was.

"Why," said he, "it's heavy as lead and white as wax! Your hand, lieutenant, appears to be completely dead;" and he looked into the eyes of the unfortunate man with an expression of profound sympathy on his face.

"Yes, I know it is, doctor, but it has been so before, and has been cured for a time, and I think can be cured again."

"Ah, indeed! Who attended you before, lieutenant?"

"Doctor ——," was the reply.

"What did he prescribe?" continued the doctor.

"Brandy," moaned the patient, to smother his desire to laugh.

"Brandy! Well, that's curious! How soon does it operate?"

"Sometimes in an hour, sometimes in two; generally in an hour."

The doctor let go his hold of the hand, and, going to a large black bottle, poured out a good half glass, at the same time saying, "There, take that." The officer took the glass and hastily swallowed its contents. He then got up, and was moving away, when the doctor said, "Call in again in a couple of hours, and let us see what effect the medicine has."

The lieutenant bowed and passed out.

"A very curious case, indeed," muttered the doctor, as he resumed his pill and quinine operations. In about two hours his patient again presented himself, showed his hand, and the doctor found it was all right.

"Well, that's *devilish* curious," quoth the doctor. "In all my experience, and it's not a short one, I never met a parallel case. Brandy has many peculiar properties which are as yet undiscovered; but in a case of complete paralysis I never knew its power as an important curative, or even such an auxiliary as it has proved in your case. The examination of the paralysis and the healing properties of brandy, as applied to the disease, would, I think, throw a new light on science, and, if you have no objection, I will convene a meeting of the surgeons of the brigade upon this most astonishing case, the result of which I will submit to the medical director of the corps."

"Doctor," returned the audacious wag, "to benefit science I would undergo any experiment upon the unfortunate limb; and I heartily assure you, that whenever the consultation is called I shall be entirely at your service."

The doctor produced the coveted brandy, and another libation was had in honor of the unfortunate member.

The hour appointed by the doctor (who was to throw new light on science) for consultation arrived. The surgeons of the brigade and some officers were assembled at his quarters. The doctor then sent his "dark Adolphus" to the quarters of the officer owning the extraordinary limb. Our boy returned with a package and a note. The doctor seized the note with some astonishment, tore it open, and began to read it. As he went on an expression of blank dismay came into his countenance. At last he flung down the note with an expression of rage. "One of ours" picked it up, and read aloud,—

My dear Doctor: I have been called hurriedly away, and cannot attend the consultation which is "destined to throw so much light on science." I forward you the limb which you say is in a state of complete paralysis. I trust, when you have carefully examined it, you will "strike" the before-mentioned "light." I hope also that you will demonstrate to the satisfaction of the wise men assembled that "brandy" has many peculiar properties which are as yet "*undiscovered*," and which, I may say, so far as *your* brandy is concerned, will remain undiscovered. Thanking you for your kindness to me while under your care, and with many compliments upon the goodness of your brandy,

    I am, my dear doctor,

        Yours truly obliged,

            LIEUTENANT ———."

The loud roars of laughter which followed the reading of the note and the examination of the package would be impossible to describe, and for several minutes the doctor's tent was in a great uproar. The doctor himself finally joined in, and in a little while resumed his good humor, and sent for the successful wag. He then produced the article containing so many "undiscovered properties." It is unnecessary to add that the consultation was eminently satisfactory, and we think the disciples of Galen went away in a slightly "obfuscated" state.

CHAPTER XVII.

How the Soldier leaves an old Camp. — Maryland Heights. — A Night March. — Harper's Ferry. — Surrounding Prospect. — John Brown's House. — Snicker's Gap. — We march to Warrenton. — McClellan superseded. — Stoneman's Station.

WE broke camp at Sharpsburg on the 30th of October, and prepared to march to Harper's Ferry, distant about twenty-five miles. We started about seven o'clock in the evening, leaving the camp, as is usual on a move, ablaze with innumerable fires, composed of superfluous firewood, old boxes, barrels, in fact, everything burnable that can be collected, which is generally piled on until mountains of flame appear in every direction. We have noticed, as a rule, that our "boys" seemed to derive much pleasure in accelerating the work of the devouring elements, and merry groups would vie with each other in making the most extensive conflagration, while loud bursts of laughter would greet the fall of an artfully-constructed pile, driving the assembled groups in all ways, merrily shouting their satisfaction, though the smoke and sparks of fire seemingly enveloped them. Our long line of men moved rapidly across the fields for the main road, and marching through Antietam, we shaped our course for Maryland Heights. The greater portion of our way was along a deep valley, through high, shelving rocks, which towered on either side, boldly standing out in strong relief against the sky, massive and jagged,— while here and there a shrub or stunted tree peeped out, as if clinging nervously to its strong protector.

> "The mountain mist took form and limb
> Of noontide hag or goblin grim."

The fires that blazed along the road, lighted by the troops which had preceded us, lit up the gigantic rocks, boldly developing the fantastic curves and crags, shaping them into giants, pygmies, and strange wild, weird shapes, and then flickering them into confused and indistinct shadows, and dark, sombre masses, at times concealing even the rough surface of the rock around and about which the reflection of the firelight played so many curious antics; in fact, our whole line of march was replete with beautiful night scenes, which called forth, at times, even from the least enthusiastic, many expressions of surprise and admiration.

The sharp, clear air, and the exhilarating influence of the varied associations, seemed to inspire our lads with extraordinary alertness: quickly we stepped forward over the rocky road, passed narrow streams at a bound, and, merrily trudging along, reached Maryland Heights about midnight, unrolled our blankets, and composed ourselves to sleep.

Early in the morning, while the sun was lingering in loving dalliance with the beautiful Aurora, our regiment was on the move. The morning was supremely beautiful; a light wind was blowing from the west, and the clear air, impregnated with the delicious aroma of flowers, gratefully saluted our nostrils, and imperceptibly seemed to endue us with vigor, so that we all started forward in great spirits, and with jokes, songs, and merry laughter, gayly went on our way, and reached Harper's Ferry about ten o'clock. As we emerged from the ravine-like road which let us out from Maryland, and left us on its border, we beheld the rapid torrent of the Potomac, rushing down before us, and its shallower parts presenting a ruin of pontoon trains, which had been destroyed by the rebels upon their rapid and disastrous retreat from Maryland. We beheld the wreck of an immense fabric, which had once been a splendid bridge, broken, dismantled, and hanging over the river, in ruins which proclaimed its former architectural beauty.

The government iron works on the Maryland side had also felt the mutilating hand of the "chivalrous" invader; but his hurried retreat prevented the disastrous consummation he so devoutly wished; and while one wing of the extensive range of buildings lay in inglorious ruin and confusion, the other stood up, tough, strong, and mighty, untouched, like the fabled Achilles after his encounter with Hector.

We looked across the Potomac, which is here about two hundred feet wide, and beheld the ruins of Harper's Ferry. We gazed around: on the Maryland side there lay heaps of railroad material, in indescribable confusion — sleepers, heaps of broken cars, piles of brick and stone, and every kind of building material, which the rebels had vainly attempted to destroy, but which, owing to the huge quantities, they had only succeeded in scattering about. Bolivar and Loudon

Heights arose before us in their stateliness and grandeur, and painfully reminded us of the disgraceful surrender that had been consummated there but a few days before, which had allowed the decimated, routed army of Lee to evade the grasp of the victorious McClellan.

A long, dirty, dusty street reached along close to the margin of the river, through which a railroad track was laid; a few straggling wooden houses were located on one side, and every one of these shanties boasted a sign, the burden of which was, "BRED AN PI HERE TO SELL," the parsimonious inhabitants charging the most exorbitant prices for the slimmest kind of pies, and introducing the purchaser to a species of small beer termed "pop," which, when it had ceased to effervesce, left the tumbler in its original state— empty! This place we thought might with propriety be termed "the withered edge of Maryland." The hot noonday sun streamed down upon us, as we sat by the railroad track waiting our turn to cross over the pontoon bridge which was laid to the other side. After clambering with much difficulty, we reached Harper's Ferry proper; and, losing the river from our view, saw the spot where John Brown, of martyred memory, made his last stand when hunted by the militia of the witless Wise.

The house, a small wooden building, was fast falling to pieces; at one end the remains of an immense chimney could be seen, which, in its original state, must have been larger than the dwelling itself. A broken fence surrounded the ruin where the gallant Brown, with a few comrades, defied a large number of the militia of Virginia, but was overcome by superior force, and reluctantly compelled to yield. The main street was composed of numerous brick houses, nearly all of which had been converted into hospitals, barracks, and provost marshals' offices; patented wooden houses were set up on the vacant lots, from which sutlers peddled their shop-worn goods, doing a double trade, taking in soldiers and greenbacks at the same time. Furloughed and wounded officers and men were staying throughout the town, and we saw many stragglers belonging to the regiments which had preceded us. Resuming our march, we left Harper's Ferry behind us. Our regiment — in fact, the whole army — were in the finest spirits, flushed as they seemed to be by their recent victories; and under the leadership of their favorite, General McClellan, they began to feel invincible. We passed regiments on the road as light-hearted and cheerful as ourselves, and at nightfall we encamped a few miles from the town.

The next morning we resumed our march, and in the afternoon reached a place called Snicker's Gap, in the Blue Ridge Mountains, and, establishing ourselves, remained there for four days, expecting that the enemy would endeavor to force the passage of the gap. This movement, however, was not attempted; owing, we suppose, to the large force upon the north side, where a considerable part of the army of the Potomac was in position. The progress of the rebels having made the defence of the "Gap" of little or no importance, we prepared to move; and started on the morning of November 6, and after wearily marching for about three days, we arrived at Warrenton, Virginia, where we encamped on the 10th of November, 1862. Here the army of the Potomac received information of the removal of General McClellan, who was superseded by General Burnside. This information, though it caused considerable disappointment, did not in the slightest degree affect the *morale* of the army.

From Warrenton we soon afterwards marched to Hartwood Church, and from thence to Stoneman's Station, near Falmouth, Virginia. These marches were devoid of interest, save in the following laughable incident, which we relate to show the legal ingenuity of the soldiers when foraging : —

When General Butler called slaves " contraband," he did the nation a service which is, I think, as yet unappreciated. That word expressed to the government and people a principle upon which to act in dealing with the slaveholders. That is a serious matter. *This* is a true one. The soldiers were really anxious, inasmuch as chickens would be seized any how, as occasion required, to find some *principle* upon which the seizure could be made. There was a Butler in the ranks, and, growing great with the occasion, he solemnly pronounced that all the chickens in Virginia were *wild*.

In pursuance of this law of war, a soldier, boldly penetrating a Virginian farm-yard, seized and put firmly under his left arm the soundest and blackest pullet in the lot. Hearing the noise consequent upon this seizure of her *wild* fowl, the woman of the house rushed out, exclaiming,

"You miserable Yankee! You've got my favorite. You're no gentleman." The soldier took the position of "front," his feet apart and at a wide brace; then thrusting his two hands into his pockets, and shifting a little the position of his left arm, so as to assure himself of a safe purchase on the chicken, as Moore says of Feramorz in Lalla Rookh, "he thus began:" "Madam, your first proposition is not true; your second may be correct; your third I admit; but while I admit that I am no 'gentleman,' I want you to acknowledge that I am a *d———d good judge of poultry!*"

The cold weather now was well upon us, and, after the hard marching and fighting of the summer, we expected soon to be ordered into winter quarters.

CHAPTER XVIII.

The Siege of Fredericksburg. — The gallant Irish Brigade. — First Day. — The Second Day. — In Position. — General Humphrey. — Expectation. — We sleep on the Field.

WE remained in camp at Falmouth a few days, while General Burnside was perfecting his plans for the siege of Fredericksburg, which commenced on the 11th of December, 1862. The siege guns of the army of the Potomac, in position on elevated points on the right and left of the houses of Phillips and De Lacey, opening fire upon the city, and continuing, for nearly three days, to hurl into the devoted city their tremendous missiles of destruction. Our engineers were desperately striving, under the cover of our guns, to lay a pontoon bridge, over which our army was to pass; and time after time they were repelled by the galling fire of musketry from the rebels in the rifle-pits on the banks of the river. But our men still continued their work, and, driving their boats upon the opposite bank, they sprang at the pits, and a fierce contest ensued, which resulted in the flight of the enemy, who rapidly retreated to the city, where again they made a stand.

The work of laying the bridges was soon effected, and a Massachusetts and a Michigan regiment passed over directly in front of the city, for the purpose of attacking it. After a brisk engagement, these regiments drove the rebels from the city to the hills beyond. A fierce fire from the artillery of the enemy, which was in position on these eminences, was then opened, and shell and shot flew thick and fast, but did not succeed in dislodging these gallant fellows. A strong force was then sent to support these two regiments, crossing the Potomac by pontoon bridges on the right and left of the city. The famous Irish Brigade formed a part of this force, and they no sooner reached the opposite side than they received orders to charge.

Posted in front of St. Mary's Heights, a position of great natural strength, and under a heavy fire, this famous brigade moved, under the leadership of the brave and accomplished Meagher, forward on their errand of death: up the steep hills, like lions they dashed upon the almost impregnable works of the foe; they fell fast, dead and dying, under the red blaze of the cannon. Again and again did they manfully try to force the Heights; time after time did they rally and again dash forward; but their devotion was in vain. The continuous artillery as well as musketry fire made fearful havoc in their ranks; and, exhausted by their herculean efforts to subjugate this stronghold, they were compelled to fall back and re-form at the foot of the hill. The fighting was continued in all parts of the field, and when night came on, and hostilities had ceased for that day, we had gained little or no material advantage.

The next day our regiment crossed, under cover of our batteries. The wounded of the Irish Brigade were down at the river side, waiting to be taken across, and were greeted with cheers by our lads as we passed, and many a stout fellow with the green boxwood in his cap looked at our Green Flag and our long lines with pitiful eyes, fearing that few of us would ever return. But the laugh and joke went round among us with the same ease and freedom as they ever did in camp. We were all in the best spirits. It was not for the regiment which had been baptized in the battles of the peninsula to feel otherwise.

We marched from the beach up the hill leading to the town and soon found ourselves in a long, narrow street. Here Colonel Guiney gave orders to unsling knapsacks. This was done; the men fell into their places. The colonel gave the command, "Load!" The guns were loaded. "Right face!" "Double-quick! March!" were the orders that next fell upon our ears; we passed through a couple of desolate streets, and in a few moments found ourselves in a large, unsheltered plain, and bullets and shells keeping high festival in the air.

We halted by order for a moment, then marched slowly and steadily by the right flank farther across the plain, crossing a small gully in which lay several bodies. Having marched a sufficient distance in the estimation of a Pennsylvania colonel who commanded our brigade, we again changed our flank, and moved in line of battle up the hill, the regiment behaving splendidly. By order of the brigade commander we again halted under a tempest of bullets and shells, and remained again inactive for several minutes.

Up to this time a number of our men had been wounded. While in this position, a regiment, or the remainder of one, came scattering in, which was the same regiment, we afterwards learned, that retreated at Boteler's Mills. They had scarcely passed, when the noble General Humphrey, hat in hand, rode up to the very top of the hill, and remained there for a few seconds in the face of a destructive fire, and under the eyes of the enemy's sharpshooters, and then rode slowly back unharmed. We remained on the hill for a time, the front regiment of the brigade, with the exception of the Fourth Michigan, being jumbled together in some confusion behind, when again we received orders to march by the left flank. All this waste of time chafed Colonel Guiney and his officers exceedingly. We moved by the flank, however, and were then ordered to march in line of battle up the hill, to take a position at the crest, and hold it. This was definite, and promised something exciting; so, on we went through the enemy's fire, cutting down and dashing through wire fences, until we gained the brow of the hill. Our flags were driven into the ground, and with our colors fluttering defiance in front of the enemy, we lay down, leaving the bullets to whistle harmlessly over our heads. We lay in this position, expecting every moment orders to charge the stone wall from behind which Ewell's division was doing such tremendous execution. But they did not come. Night gradually fell upon us; the roar of artillery ceased; the roll of musketry gradually died away; and at dark all was still. The shouts of the rebels, who were but a few hundred yards from us, could be heard, and the groans of their wounded; ours had been taken to the city, and across the river. Their camp fires could be seen; we had none burning: amid the carnage and destruction that reigned around, we lay in our blankets, and many of us slept.

11

CHAPTER XIX.

The Continuation of the Siege. — Very near. — It takes an Irishman to crack a Joke. — Our hopeless Position. — We evacuate the Heights. — The sacked City. — How to be jolly under any Circumstances. — A Presentation. — We return to Falmouth.

THE next morning (Sunday) was bright and clear, and the terrible conflict of the previous day was resumed. The artillery roared along the line, and the fierce musketry fires of the contending forces made the din almost indescribable. A Massachusetts volunteer regiment near us kept up a continuous fire; for what purpose no one could tell, for it is our conviction that not one shot out of the eighty rounds per man that was fired, did any execution. It served to draw the terrific fire of the enemy upon us, and to render our position very dangerous and uncomfortable. This we should not have cared so much about if we had had a chance to return their fire effectively; but, sheltered as the enemy were by an almost impregnable stone wall, it was impossible to do so. However, the regiment kept up its fire, and did not cease until every man had expended his ammunition. Had the enemy then charged on them they could not have repulsed them for want of ammunition. Orders had been sent to them several times to cease firing; but we suppose the near proximity of the enemy, though defended by a stone wall, was too tempting an opportunity to be passed by such enterprising marksmen.

The Ninth kept their place upon the hill in full enjoyment of their *otium cum dignitate*. Many of the officers surrounded Colonel Guiney, smoking, telling stories, cracking jokes, and perpetrating such conundrums as would win the envy of Joe Miller, were he then in the land of the living. Whiz — whiz — came the bullets, without cessation, hundreds of times unpleasantly close to us; but the puns *would* come, the joke *would* be cracked, the story told, notwithstanding the authors thereof stood a most likely chance to be hit by the deadly missiles that were flying around.

If we remember aright, a great deal of tobacco was consumed that day; and one soldier had his pipe knocked from his mouth by a bullet. This was a great misfortune, as pipes were very scarce, and the poor fellow could not borrow another.

Whilst we lay upon this hill the firing continued very heavily, and we were anxiously expecting orders to charge the enemy, when, looking around, we noticed a tall, stout fellow of our regiment, whom we had remarked some few minutes before, calmly sleeping amid the crashing and roaring around, start up from his slumbers, with a cry of pain, and pressing his arm, moan piteously. "Arrah, hold yer whist!" cried a companion near; "the bullet didn't hurt ye — look at that!" and taking his cap from his head, he took the ball from the inside! It seems the bullet had glanced from the arm of the sleeper and perforated the cap of his comrade, whose head was lying in close proximity to his companion's elbow.

The colonel of the One Hundred and Tenth Pennsylvania happened to be looking at him, and when he saw the bullet, remarked, "Well, it takes an Irishman to crack a joke."

We lay on the hill that day, chafing with impatience for a more active part in the battle then fiercely raging. Many of our men were hit, and sometimes wounded as badly as though in the midst of the conflict, and we were in infinitely greater danger from the explosion of the shells than if farther in the front. However, there we were ordered to remain. We must curb our impatience, and, if we could not actively participate in, await the issue of the conflict.

It was now evident to the soldiers of the army of the Potomac, that, however well they might fight, whatever valor they might display, this great assault would be attended with only one result — the falling back of our entire army. The Heights of Fredericksburg, of immense natural strength, were strongly supported both by artillery and infantry; and Lee having the best position it was possible to select, could easily repel the onslaught of our troops with a much smaller force of his own. On the other hand, our forces were massed upon his front, literally piled up before him, and from their unscientific and circumscribed position, one half of our army paralyzed the other. The attack upon the enemy's works was continued throughout the day, our artillery on the right doing splendid execution. The forces upon the flank of our line, under

Franklin, had thrice unsuccessfully assaulted the works of the enemy, but the blinding storm of bullets, grape, and shrapnel mowed down the gallant regiments as they advanced, literally destroying them before they reached the works. Yet still the hopeless task was continued. The brave men of our army moved steadily in the footsteps of those that had fallen only to share their fate. Thus regiment after regiment, brigade after brigade, and division after division, moved forward to play their *rôle* in the mighty tragedy that was being enacted, until the curtain of night dropped, and closed the bloody and heart-rending scene. On that terrible Sunday night we knew that the army of the Potomac had been repulsed. Orderlies and staff officers passed swiftly to and fro over the field; whispered orders passed rapidly from mouth to mouth; messengers flitted from regiment to regiment in the darkness. Suddenly, the whole army arose. Silently the men rolled up their blankets and prepared to move. Shortly before midnight the repulsed columns moved back toward the city. The Heights had been evacuated. The great sacrifice of human lives had been in vain.

It was about midnight when we entered the city. We found several divisions of the army already assembled there. Stacks of arms lined both sides of the street. Along the sidewalks were stretched hundreds of weary soldiers, sleeping in their blankets, while here and there a form rolled in a shelter-tent, which had originally been white, presented, in the misty light, a spectral looking appearance. Flickering lights could be seen slowly moving in the streets, and here and there dingy lights lit up dingy corners, seemingly increasing the gloom. From the windows of large buildings calm, steady lights struggled faintly forth, and the passenger, looking up from the street, could discern that they were full of sick and wounded; while in the steadily-moving figures shadowed forth could be plainly seen surgeons and nurses as they tended the poor soldier. In the entries of houses dead and wounded were lying on stretchers. The dead had been brought in from the field alive, but had since expired. Wagons stood in the streets, from which rations were being issued to the tired and hungry men who had come in from the front. Bread was not weighed out there; it was "take what you want." The store doors were wide open, and broken boxes and barrels, weights, scales, and destroyed goods of all kinds flung recklessly around. Soldiers, with bits of tallow candles in their powder-begrimed hands, were prying into the different apartments in search of spoil. Some were pulling up the flooring in search of treasure, which they imagined was secreted everywhere; some were sounding the walls around; others, standing on the end of a barrel, were holding a mimic auction, and disposing of coats and waistcoats at "ruinous sacrifices" to the laughing and admiring crowd. Others, of a literary turn, were deciphering accounts from great ledgers and entry books, and commenting on the lucky situation of John Doe, who was the debtor of Richard Roe to an immense amount. More were counting out large piles of Virginia bank notes of which the bank next door had been despoiled. Here and there you could see a waggish fellow, in female attire, strutting about on the arm of a comrade, and, daintily lifting his skirts, exposing a tremendous ankle clad in an unromantic government shoe. We watched these scenes a little while, and then moved away in search of more aristocratic quarters; and these were plenty. We found a fine dwelling, with the windows standing invitingly open. We tried the door; it yielded. Entering a fine hall, a side-door led us into a splendidly-furnished parlor; a rich carpet was on the floor; a well-filled book-case against the wall; a comfortable sofa and numerous easy chairs were disposed about the room. We let down the curtains, and locked the door. One of "ours" went to a fine piano, opened it, and, seating himself, gave us snatches from *Il Trovatore, La Sonnambula, Le Prophete, Der Freyschutz,* and gliding from *Traviata,* to the dashing melody of the "*Bowld Soger Boy,*" an hour or two passed merrily in music and song; then the piano was closed, and, after a brief examination of the house, which belonged to Dr. ——, we lay down on the soft carpet, and soon were buried in sleep.

Early the next morning we strolled about the city, and went to the quarters of the remnant of the famous Irish Brigade. They were down by the river side, and we found the havoc made among their ranks to be worse than we anticipated. Later in the day, our officers received a cordial invitation to witness the presentation of a stand of new colors, given to the Irish Brigade by the ladies of New York, which took place in the theatre of Fredericksburg, and, considering the surrounding oppressive circumstances, passed off with considerable *eclat*. After the presentation, on returning to our comfortable quarters, news greeted us that our regiment was to be again ordered to the front. Hour after hour passed away, however, and still no orders came. At last we retired to rest. About midnight we were aroused, and the regiment began to move. We imagined we were going to the front, and not until we arrived at the pontoon did we discover that Fredericksburg was being evacuated. We crossed the river that night, and, after a weary march, reached our old camp at Stoneman's Station, Falmouth, as the day was breaking.

At Fredericksburg, Burnside suffered in more respects than one. When that unfortunate battle was over, we re-crossed the Rappahannock, and while engaged in the weary process of retreat, a long and inexplicable halt occurred on the bridge, the commanding general reminding me of Swaran in the ancient poem of Cath-Loda, when " slowly stealing over the stream, he whistled as he went."

CHAPTER XX.

Winter Quarters. — Those Pies. — Punch. — The Child of the Forest. — A Reconnoissance to Barnett's Ford. — Sharp Marching. — Horse-racing. — How we spent St. Patrick's Day. — Fatal Accident.

HAVING again settled ourselves down at Falmouth, in front of Fredericksburg, we cast about for something to vary the monotony of camp life. The first thing to be done, however, was to prepare for winter, which was now upon us. We therefore went to work, erected log foundations over deep cellars, fixed our wall and shelter tents upon them, devised and built practicable fireplaces with mud chimneys, and soon began to feel very comfortable. Sutlers, which the majority of our fellows, to this day, call "Settlers," and purveyors swarmed about the camp, and all kinds of articles, edible, useful, and ornamental, could be purchased of them by paying unheard-of prices. Bakeries were established with "patent ovens," invented by some enterprising genius in New York, who supplied soft bread to the troops. These bakers received their flour from the government, and in making the bread they managed, likewise, to make a large percentage. "Cute" men, hearing of the great success of the "patent ovens," determined to come down to Falmouth from Washington and start opposition bakeries. A number of them came down and manufactured pies. "Pies" — that was the sweet, luscious appellation given to some flat circular pieces of paste, baked brown, in one of the said ovens. A few bites off one of the pies would bring you to a few berries, of what kind the soldiers have never discovered; and after curiously examining these hidden mysteries, finding they could make nothing of them, it was deemed best to press them into the crust and swallow them incontinently. Gradually the sutlers and purveyors became more enterprising, and would bring down ale, &c.; the advent of the beer, we know, was a joyful occasion; we had not tasted any for more than a year, and as this was remarkably good, it was received and drank with a great deal of satisfaction.

Our evenings in camp were spent cheerfully

and pleasantly. Before a blazing fire of no ordinary dimensions, half a dozen of us would be seated under the canvas shelter in front, watching with profound interest the solemn and systematic proceedings of one of "ours." From one pocket he would take a few lemons, which he would place, with considerable dignity, upon the bed. Then, stooping down and making a few vigorous dives under that rustic couch, he would reappear with two or three suspicious-looking canteens; these, with a mysterious wink, he would deposit beside the lemons; this done, half a dozen anxious voices would cry out simultaneously, "Harry!" The individual addressed, whose optics were rather sharp, and whose sense of smell was rather keen, would unthinkingly expose his proximity by instantaneously introducing his head through the partial opening in the tent. "Well, gemmen?" "Bring — the — sugar — Harry — and — one spoon — and, my 'Child of the Forest,' be expeditious!" Harry was commonly known as the Child of the Forest. He looked more like a victim fresh from the rack. He was a huge, ungainly, loose-jointed fellow, and always, when walking, seemed to proceed sideways, like a rooster preparing to fight. Well,

Harry would produce the sugar from some mysterious corner, which was placed beside the other necessaries. Then a few anxious voices would insinuatingly hint, for the edification of one of our circle (who had joined the Child of the Forest within), "I'd make it pretty strong, Nick, if I were you." "O, yes," the balance would chorus, "make it hot and strong;" and then another ominous silence would ensue, every eye being bent on the dignified compounder. Soon the mysterious decoction would be completed; then half a dozen drinking tins would be filled with the steaming and fragrant beverage yclept "punch," and soon, very soon, emptied, — Harry looking on at the rapid consumption with what we should imagine to be a fair resemblance of the grin of a pleased demon displayed on his huge face; and with a chuckle, would turn about and shuffle away to his cook-house, hidden in some remote part of which he would watch the advent of some daring fellow who would come to abstract some of the articles of the mess, and, when he appeared, pounce on him with a tragic growl, and a "I've got yer now!" but sometimes, before he had concluded the sentence, he would be knocked into a kettle of his own soup!

A draught from the steaming jug of punch completely changed the scene. Good humor sparkled forth on every face, the bright glow from the fire seeming to increase in warmth, till we moved back our seats, and threw ourselves into more comfortable attitudes. Conversation would soon merge into relations of adventure, surmises as to pending movements, home, friends, and country; occasionally the narratives would take a cheerful tone, then melancholy, and at times even terrible; and, amid a breathless silence, the narrator would proceed till our interest had been thoroughly excited, and then abruptly stop; and we all laughed merrily to think that we had so soon been interested; then songs would be sung, — for many of our circle were good singers; then came solos, glees, quartets, and choruses, that would, for power and energy, if not for melody, rival the elaborate concerts of our own dear little city of Boston.

Thus the time passed on, varied by some slight marches and reconnoissances. One of the latter we well remember: it was made by our brigade, under the command of General Barnes, to Kelley's Ford, on the other side of which the rebels were in force, having rifle-pits upon the banks of the river.

We started early on the morning of December 30, and, after marching rapidly many miles, halted for the night; and, as we could not light fires for fear of attracting the attention of the enemy, we were compelled to go to bed supperless, but, being very weary, slept soundly. A very heavy mist fell during the night, and when we awoke in the morning our blankets were saturated. We continued our march, and reached the ford, our cavalry, who were in advance of us, capturing four or five rebels. Having accurately ascertained the enemy's position, we started back the same morning for our camp: continuing on our way, our men showing evident signs of exhaustion, we arrived near Harwood Church, ten miles from our camp. Here choice was given us, either to encamp for the night, or march onward to camp. After some consideration, the decision was, "keep on:" this we did, and reached our quarters at Falmouth about eight o'clock. That reconnoissance was the hardest march performed by any brigade in the army of the Potomac. We marched fifty-four miles in less than thirty-one hours; deducting from that the eight or nine hours we rested on the first night, there will be left, we think, a record of endurance highly creditable to those who took part therein.

After this tough sample of military labor, we were allowed to rest, and pass away the time as best we could. One of our principal sources of amusement was horse-racing. The regiment boasted many remarkable specimens of horse flesh, all of them being, in the estimation of their owners, something extraordinary. Among these was one called the "*Cat*," which, in the language of one of our men, "wasn't much to look at, but the devil's own boy to go." Where the Cat came from, to whom he belonged, or where he finally went, nobody knows. Dr. Ryan, however, introduced him to our regimental turf; the doctor swore that the Cat was sired by one of the best stallions in the country, and foaled by a mare that would knock bright spots out of Flora Temple. As the doctor was "up" on horse flesh, no one contradicted him; but when they went away they would silently gyrate their thumbs upon the nose and invest their pile upon the other side. Ryan generally rode the Cat, and by some hocus-pocus always managed to come in ahead. So it was that the fame of the wretched-looking Cat went up. There was another noted horse we saw there, rejoicing in the modest appellation of the "*War Horse.*" Tradition said he was very fast, but the old fellow never would *verify* tradition. He was matched against the Cat, but the tremendous gap intervening between the latter and himself completely destroyed his reputation for fleetness. It is but justice, however, to the old War Horse, to say, that he always held his character for being a "fast eater."

Many very fine races were run there, however, in which the horses of General Griffin, our division commander, took part; the white Arabian of Colonel Guiney; the fine animal "Dick" of Lieutenant-Colonel Hanley; and, between horses, the property of other officers of the brigade. Very exciting times we used to have; and the brigade would turn out *en masse* to witness these racing carnivals, which helped to pass time pleasantly away.

In this manner we jogged along until the month of March, when we began to make preparations for the celebration of St. Patrick's Day. Arrangements on an extensive scale were made for a pleasant celebration. "Goodies" were brought from Washington by the sutlers, and a large wall tent erected, in which, after the festivities of the day, the officers and their friends and guests were to assemble and spend the evening. The morning of the 17th came upon us bright, beautiful, and bracing, and found the camp in a fine state of cleanliness, and tastefully decorated with evergreens and appropriate mottoes. A tall pole was erected on a vacant spot, opposite the regimental quarters, which was thickly greased: on the top of the pole was a furlough paper for ten days, which was to be the prize for the successful climber. A number of candidates appeared, and about ten o'clock in the morning, these slippery ascensions commenced. One tall, stout fellow made a desperate effort to lift himself from the ground, and, after trying for about half an hour, was reluctantly compelled to give it up, having in that time only achieved about an inch; he looked wistfully at the paper fluttering above him, and then turned away to give room to an ambitious youngster, who succeeded in getting half way up, when, coming to a spot greasier than the rest, he began to slip, and did not pause until he came to ground, amid the roars of the crowd.

Several other enterprising spirits attempted the task, but the pole slipped through their hands, and the furlough fluttered tauntingly above them, until, at last, no more could be found to make the attempt, and then the crowd adjourned to the race ground, where several fast runners were in line; an exciting race was then run, when the grand event of the day came off — a horse-race, in which several of the fastest horses of the brigade were entered. It was in this race that Quartermaster Thomas Mooney received the fearful injuries which eventually terminated his life.

This unfortunate occurrence closed the festivities, and cast a shadow over the spirits of us all. Lieutenant Mooney was highly respected by his associates, and was a genial, warm-hearted man, and the sad termination of his life was deeply regretted. Every care was bestowed on him by the surgeons and his brother officers, but all in vain; he died shortly afterwards, and his remains were conveyed to his home in Boston.

The Irish Brigade, at this time, was encamped about two miles from us; they also had a grand celebration, at which General Hooker was present; some splendid samples of horse flesh were brought upon the ground, and, in addition to flat races, a steeple chase was run in presence of an immense assemblage.

That winter at Falmouth was the most genial and comfortable one we ever spent; and, after the toil of marches and the ordeal of battles, we gladly look back on it with feelings of pleasurable satisfaction.

CHAPTER XXI.

The Regiment is presented with a new Flag. — We leave Falmouth. — Kelley's Ford. — Ellis' Ford. — The Battle of Chancellorsville. — The Plank Road. — A wrong Turn. — How the Doctors were routed. — Ellis' Ford. — Sketch of Mr. Ellis. — To Brandy Station. — Encounter with the Enemy. — Tough Marching. — Bad Luck to this Marching.

WHILE at this camp we were highly honored by the presentation to our regiment of a splendid green flag, of great value, by the Irish brigade. The names of all the battles we had passed through were inscribed on the face of it in letters of gold, while, on the reverse, a large gold harp was embroidered of exquisite beauty and workmanship.

This gratifying presentation took place in the centre of a square formed by our regiment, and the flag was turned over to Colonel P. R. Guiney by General Meagher, in one of those magnificent rhetorical efforts for which he is distinguished, and appropriately responded to by Colonel Guiney in the name of the regiment.

Battle of Chancellorsville.

The remainder of the winter months soon passed away. General Burnside, having resigned his command, was succeeded by General Hooker, and preparations were then made for a spring campaign, which culminated in the battle of Chancellorsville.

On the 27th of April, our army, under the command of General Hooker, moved from Falmouth in the direction of Kelley's Ford, on the Rappahannock, which we crossed, surprising the enemy and driving him back upon the formidable works in his rear. The army then crossed the Rapidan, at Ellis' Ford, and marched to a place called Chancellorsville, in Orange County, Virginia. Here we halted, and soon our forces were in position, and prepared to give battle to General Lee. The engagement was commenced by the artillery of the Union troops, which kept up a continuous fire throughout the day. The Fifth Corps, under the command of General Sykes, commenced the conflict, and succeeded in driving the rebel force from its position. A large number of the Zouaves, a fine regiment from New York, were killed and wounded. They fought magnificently that day, and succeeded in maintaining the position they had so bravely won. The Ninth, upon the extreme left of the right wing, had thrown up strong breastworks facing the enemy's centre, which they had been instructed to maintain to the death.

The columns of Jackson, escaping the clutch of Sedgwick, at Fredericksburg, changed the face of affairs, however, making it necessary for our division to leave their works, and march on the plank road to intercept Jackson, and keep him from the field until the forces of Lee, in the front, were beaten by General Hooker. By some mistake upon the part of subordinate commanders, a wrong route was taken, and Jackson, in full possession of the plank road, marched without interruption to the support of Lee, and succeeded in repulsing the main force of Hooker, compelling him to take up a new position on the fields in front of Chancellorsville House, where a portion of our artillery was posted, and about a quarter of a mile in the rear of our original line. The fine fighting of our troops, however, preserved all our original advantages of position, and the general feeling among them was, that Lee would be defeated. The movements of General Hooker were characterized by celerity and decision, and the troops had the fullest confidence in his ability; and, being in the best of spirits, the defeat of the rebels was anticipated. From prisoners that were captured we learned that the rapid movements of Hooker had taken Lee completely by surprise; and many of them further remarked that we had " taken the right way to master Lee;" in fact, they all seemed to believe that Chancellorsville was the beginning of the last days of the Confederacy.

Our regiment was engaged a great part of the time in supporting Griffin's battery and doing picket duty. Two of the companies of our regiment, while on picket, were engaged with the enemy, and handsomely repulsed him. The battle of Chancellorsville occupied about three days, when General Hooker found it necessary to fall back, the army crossing safely at the United States Ford on the morning of May 5, having marched all night without being harassed by Lee's forces, to whom our retreat was entirely unexpected.

The battle cost a great many lives, and following as it did upon the heels of Fredericksburg, seemed to leave our army in a very bewildered state. They could scarcely understand how these consecutive defeats had occurred, after all the splendid fighting they had done and the extraordinary marches they had performed. We are reminded of an incident of that battle which may be worth relating. We were engaged on the provost guard, of the First Division, Fifth Army Corps, and we had charge of a number of rebel prisoners who had been taken in the first day's fighting. When this division moved in the direction of the plank road, so called, one of the prisoners remarked to us, " You are going to intercept Jackson; you have missed him, however; while you are marching this way he is coming down the plank road, beyond those hills," pointing to a range about a quarter of a mile distant, " and will form a junction with Lee's main body before you can turn back and catch him." It proved to be very true; the junction was formed, and the army of the Potomac was repulsed.

An amusing incident came under our notice during the progress of the engagement at Chancellorsville, which may prove interesting. A large number of wounded had been brought in from the front upon stretchers, and carried to the hospital tents about a quarter of a mile in the rear. These tents were pitched in the woods, and were supposed to be out of reach of the enemy's fire. About noon, however, of the second day's fight, the heavy guns of the enemy opened fire, and threw their shells right into the wood and surrounding places.

It was a curious sight to see the wounded men, who, a moment before, seemed unable to rise up, scramble from their stretchers, and hobble farther to the rear; to see the surgeons display extraordinary agility in packing up their murderous-looking instruments, strike their tents, and follow their astonished patients to a place of greater security.

It was, "Take up thy bed and walk" most comically illustrated. The poor, wounded fellows no doubt thought that it was enough to get struck in action, without waiting to be demolished in their beds; and they were right. No one was hit, however, and they succeeded in making their retreat in good order, the soldier with his "kit," and the surgeons with their implements of torture.

On the evening of the 6th of May, the whole army, after a tiresome march over rough, muddy roads, found themselves back in their old camps, anxiously speculating as to who would be the next commander of the army of the Potomac; for, in the terse and expressive language of the Ninth, General Hooker was "certainly gone up."

On the 28th of the same month, our army was again on the move: as usual, the roads were very bad: after a march of about ten miles our regiment encamped at Harwood Church. Early the next morning the march was resumed, and, after bivouacking one or two nights, we arrived at Ellis' Ford, on the Rappahannock, and established ourselves in camp in the woods, close to the river. We then sent two companies of ours out on picket to guard the ford, and men were detailed from the remainder of the regiment to throw up breastworks along the edge of the river. The enemy, who were posted on the summit of the bluff on the opposite side, opened fire upon our working party with musketry, and afterwards brought up a piece of artillery, and fired two charges of grape and canister. Fortunately no one was hit, and our work proceeded.

The following description, from the note-book of an officer,[*] of Ellis, of Ellis' Ford, may be found interesting: —

---

[*] Notes by an officer of the regiment.

"I have not stated anything of our stay at old Ellis', at the ford, and the friendly converse maintained with him, and the inexpressible pleasure I enjoyed in sleeping on his comfortable sofa, and occasionally reclining even on his soft and downy bed. The old man, somewhat of a cripple, did not like the idea of remaining in his chamber during the night, lest an engagement might take place between the opposing forces, and an accidental shot might send him, *not* prematurely, to the dominions of Pluto; he would find himself between two fires, and the situation *might* not be considered enviable. He was, therefore, careful to vacate the premises each evening and hobble to the rear, where he found rest, and imagined he found security in the house of one of his employees. Before leaving, he would regularly hand over the key of his chamber, which was just inside the piazza, to the officer in command of the post, with liberty to enjoy the comforts of his bed or sofa. These were a rich treat to the soldier long accustomed to nothing but the greensward or hard boards; however, I always remarked I slept better on the hard boards outside on the platform of the piazza, or on the green grass, than on the old man's luxurious couch. Old Mr. Ellis is a perfect Crœsus — rich in land, money, and negroes. But I think he suffers from a want of the necessaries of life, as his supplies are, to a great extent, cut off by the occupation of his territory by the conflicting forces. He was never married. All the female society he at presents enjoys is confined to two smutty, corpulent, dirty, aged colored women, whom I, at least, would not suffer in sight. I wonder how it is that any man of respectability, feeling, or decency, can bear to be a slaveholder, while he is surrounded by such pictures of degradation and misery as many of the southern plantations present, and which should appeal to the finer feelings of his nature."

Ellis' house was situated within a few yards of the river bank, along which our forces had thrown up rifle-pits. The ford was about thirty feet wide, and the rebel picket on the other side was within speaking distance. During the daytime, no shots would be exchanged, though at night the stillness would sometimes be broken by a few straggling rifle-shots, and sometimes by a volley when the rebels apprehended an attack from our side. Nothing of interest or importance took place while we were there, the general position of the opposing forces being still the same as when we first moved down to the ford. We left that place about the 5th of June, and moved on to Kelley's Ford, and remained there for three or four days, engaged in duties similar to those at Ellis'. On the morning of the 9th we crossed the Rappahannock via Kelley's Ford, to support our cavalry, which had crossed the river in great force under Generals Gregg and Kilpatrick. They encountered the enemy near Brandy Station, some ten or fifteen thousand strong, and a fierce fight took place. The Ninth and Thirty-second Regiments were ordered farther to the front, in support of our cavalry, and we passed on for about five miles. The First Michigan followed, and protected the road over which we had passed to prevent our retreat being cut off. The cavalry engagement was commenced by a heavy artillery fire. About four o'clock the former became engaged, fighting until dark, when the enemy fell back badly beaten. Several wounded men of both sides were carried to the rear, where we were held in reserve, and they represented the fight as the greatest cavalry engagement that ever took place on this continent. The number of sabre cuts on heads and arms proclaimed the severity of the contest and the close proximity of the combatants. We returned the same night to Kelley's Ford, and marched shortly afterwards to Morrisville. From there we pushed on, and marched day after day, with irregular intervals of rest, via Warrenton, Manassas, and Centreville to Gum Springs, Aldie, Virginia. During these marches the heat was unusually oppressive; many poor fellows dropped down exhausted by the road-side. Many men died, overcome by the intolerable heat, and the weight of their knapsacks and other habiliments of a soldier. While we were marching in the direction of Bull Run, a remark reached us from one of "our" comical characters. On leaving Catlett's Station it became evident where we were bound.

"Where's the grand army going now, Pat?" queried one of the other.

"O, then, don't you know," was the reply, "we are going to Bull Run to get our *annual batin'?*"

At another time, as we were crossing the Rappahannock, a tall, strapping fellow of "ours" stopped, and suddenly laid down his gun.

"What are you doing now, Jim?" said a companion.

"O, the divil! I'm stoppin' to reorganize!" at the same time shifting his knapsack more comfortably and securely on his shoulders.

When he was "reorganized" he resumed his march, humming, —

> "Bad luck to this marching,
>   Pipe-claying and starching:
> How neat one must be to be killed by the French!
>   I'm sick of parading,
>   Through wet and cold wading,
> Or standing all night to be shot in a trench."

CHAPTER XXII.

General Meade assumes Command. — Gettysburg. — Following the Enemy. — We reënter Virginia. — The Professor's Excuse for Lagging. — He could not rob the Dead.

THE army of the Potomac was rapidly concentrated in and about Aldie, from which place General Hooker, still in command, moved his columns down in pursuit of Lee's army, which was rapidly advancing through Maryland upon Pennsylvania, to carry out his scheme of retaliation, and to encourage the great peace party, which he imagined then existed in the North, but in which he eventually found himself wofully mistaken.

We passed rapidly through the several towns and cities of Maryland, and on reaching Frederick City, Md., learned that Hooker had been relieved by General Meade. We were followed by the good wishes of nearly all the inhabitants, and on the morning of July 1 crossed the Pennsylvania state line, close upon the rear of Lee's invading army. The same night we arrived at Hanover, Pa., and encamped within a few miles of the memorable field of Gettysburg. The next day our regiment was sent on picket on the extreme right of the line of battle; but we were called in, later in the day, to participate in the great battle that was then raging; but as night was advancing, we were not very prominently exposed.

The position of the regiment was changed to the left on the 3d and 4th, and we were engaged in a heavy skirmish with the enemy in front, and succeeded in maintaining our position, though opposed by a heavy force. The position where they were placed was of great importance to the success of General Meade's plans; and the general opinion was, that if the right of Lee's army pressed their attack on this wing, the Ninth, unless strongly reënforced, would be annihilated. In fact, the regiment moved forward to their position with a sort of misgiving that we should have very hot work, and that to escape without terrific loss of life would be next to a miracle; but even this did not lessen the ardor of our brave boys, and they took their position and firmly maintained it.

The terrible onslaughts of Meade on Lee's front were of that powerful nature that demanded all of the enemy's strength to resist, and before he could well turn his attention to other sections of his elongated front, the battle had been decided and the invader ignominiously beaten; the other regiments of our brigade, detached from us, and more immediately in the midst of the fight, were terribly cut up. They fought with great gallantry, and in the midst of the dire conflict the murmur ran through their lines, "Where's the Ninth? Why have they been taken from us?" But the Ninth, solitary and alone, held their place in a distant part of the field, and *they* asked, "Where's the rest of our brigade?" The dividing of the brigade, the regiments of which had so often met the enemy side by side, caused much dissatisfaction.

It is not for us to present a picture of the terrible field of Gettysburg. We fear a true and faithful account can never be written, or the many tableaux of that panorama of brave deeds, indomitable courage, or of carnage, destruction, and terror, be depicted. The vacant chair in many a home, the seared spot on many a heart, the epitaph for many a grave, may be read in the now familiar name, "Gettsyburg;" while, towering above all, it forms a monument of Meade's genius, which will last even when the great shaft that there commemorates the dead has crumbled into dust!

General Lee, having evacuated his position and commenced his retreat, was closely followed up by our army. On the 5th of July, Kilpatrick's division of cavalry, which had been sent out early in the day, returned, and reported that Lee's army was making for Williamsport. We therefore immediately moved by way of South Mountain, passing through Boonsboro' and Temblinstown, and soon came upon the enemy in position a short distance from Williamsport, his left within a few miles of Temblinstown. Here General Meade, no doubt, expected Lee would give him battle: he therefore proceeded to strengthen his position by such fortifications as were necessary, and awaited Lee's preliminary movements. No sign, however, indicated the enemy's intentions during the night of the 13th; on the next day, on our skirmishers being deployed, and gradually contracting their lines about Williamsport, they found it to be evacuated.

Thus was the second Maryland campaign

ended, and with losses equally disastrous, if not worse than the first to the audacious Rebels.*

The army of the Potomac, on the 17th of July, inspired by the success of Gettysburg, proceeded to pay back the compliment by an invasion of their own, and, crossing the Potomac at Berlin, Maryland, they entered that barrenest of all barren states, Virginia.

We had one of those odd characters called an "Irish hedge schoolmaster" in the regiment. He was technically called the "Professor," and we think our trans-Atlantic friends will recognize him as a type of the ancient *genus*. Be his officers ever so watchful, the professor generally managed to fall out when the regiment was approaching an engagement. He did this at Gettysburg; the day after the engagement he rejoined his company, and was accosted by the colonel with,—

"Well, sir, how came you absent from the ranks?" The professor threw himself into po-

---

* The result of the campaign may be briefly stated: the defeat of the enemy at Gettysburg, their compulsory evacuation of Pennsylvania and Maryland, and withdrawal from the upper valley of the Shenandoah, and the capture of three guns, forty-one standards, and 13,621 prisoners, and 24,978 small arms collected on the battle-field. — *Extract from General Meade's Official Report.*

sition, and, having given the customary salute with considerable dignity, delivered the following characteristic explanation: —

"When within about two miles of this historic field, I fell out by the road-side for the purpose of recuperating my exhausted energies. After five hours' unruffled slumber I awoke, startled by the roaring of many batteries of artillery, and, colonel, in the weakness of my judgment, and under all the painful circumstances, I deemed it prudent to remain in the rear."

The colonel was so stunned by this lucid and grandiloquent explanation, that, to this day, no punishment for this dereliction of duty has been inflicted on the *prudent* professor.

During the first day of the battle our men were somewhat short of provisions, the wagons being some distance in the rear. After we had lain down at night, one of our fellows, more hungry and wide awake than the rest, rose, and approached a dead soldier that was near, by whose side lay a well-filled haversack: kneeling down by the body, he opened the haversack and saw, revealed by the clear light of the moon, a goodly feast of "flour rolls," looking temptingly brown and nice, which the poor fallen soldier had purchased on the march, but had not had time to eat before he was engaged in his last fight. One by one, our boy transferred them to his own haversack, and then he rose to move away. He moved about two paces, and suddenly stopped. Pausing a moment in seeming meditation, he turned round to where the dead soldier was lying, his pale face revealed by the moonlight. Our fellow kneeled gently down by his side, and one by one he took the rolls from his haversack, and placed them in that from which he had taken them: carefully drawing a blanket over the face of the dead man, he passed slowly away. The poor fellow was too conscientious to despoil the dead of his food, although himself very hungry.

Conscience vs. Hunger. Page 200

CHAPTER XXIII.

Incidents of a March. — A dirty Musket. — The Colonel and the Corporal. — An ungrateful Man. — Retaliation. — More of the Professor. — How he got his Larnin'.

THE Ninth found themselves once more in Virginia, marching over the same ground and gazing upon the same familiar scenes they had so often passed during the last two years. Not a road, not a stream, or hill, or valley, or shorn wood, but looked to them like an old friend. Here they had done picket duty on many a long night. There many a pleasant evening had been passed around that charred old stump, against which the camp fires had cheerily burned. Along that smooth, hard road, many a foot-race had been run, or many a wrestling match had been consummated. Between those little drains and ridges they had often soundly slept; and those unromantic heaps which at one time were considered an "illigant" chimney, in our not-over-fastidious estimation, could they speak, what stories they might tell of adventure, personal or romantic, told by our gossiping lads of a winter night as they sat around the cheerful fire that blazed therein! The soldier's life may not be conducive to the development of the gentler feelings of our nature. But this we do know: we have seen strong, cold-hearted men moved by such scenes as we have feebly attempted to portray, and the recurrence of so many familiar places made it seem as though the mission of the army of the Potomac was indeed circumscribed — as though their battles and bivouacs were to be fought and made in the self-same area. In a word, Virginia and its vicinity were the great book which they had long perused, the chapters of which were indelibly impressed on their memory, and every passage was to them as familiar as a song.

Our boys, as they trudged along, pointed out well-known spots; and then came quaint sayings and comical stories, in some way associated with them.

"Jimmie, d'ye remember when we was here, when the kurnel axed me what I had sich a dirty musket for, and I showed him me shovel, an' ses I, 'Kurnel, maybe the gun's a bit dirty, but this shovel's purty well polished;' 'cause I'd bin workin' at that there fort for a fortnight; an' the kurnel laughed, an' ses he to the captin, as they went away, ' P'raps, captin, that's more in his line.'" " O, yes; I remember that well, Tim," returned Jimmie, with a broad grin; " but ould Mike the corpler kot the kurnel as fine as ever he war kot in his life. Mike was on juty one day, an' he let somebody pass, what had no business to. The kurnel herd it, and when he sees the corpler he axed him ' what for he done that.' Mike said, ' 'cause he thought it war all right.' Ses the kurnel, ' Well, you're a purty feller! what confounded fool made you a corpler ?' 'Shure, kurnel,' ses Mike, '*it was yourself.*'" Roars of laughter followed this narration; then Jimmie resumed the conversation. " God be wid them times; poor Mike was a quare fellow. It war a shame he war killed the way he was. We war goin' through the wood at Malvern, jist out from the field, when we seed a wownded reb setting forenenst a tree. ' Give us a drink of water,' ses he. Ould Mike stopped and give him a drink out of his canteen, while we went on. Purty soon we herd a shot, and looked back and seed poor Mike fall. The cowardly snake had shot him after drinkin' his water.* Charley Willis run back an' dashed the butt of his musket on the rascal's head, an' settled him, the brute! Arrah, some of them war great villains, Tim."

"They war, indeed! didn't meself see 'em proddin' the wounded with their bayonets, an' robbin' 'em afore they was dead?" Here Jimmie pulled out his old black pipe, and, seizing a brand from a fire by the road-side, hastily lit it, and was about to proceed with the conversation.

"Whist!" said Tim, with a nudge of the elbow, as Jimmie was about to speak; "here's the Purfessor. We'll have some fun wid the quare divil, for he's mighty grand whin he wants to be."

The Professor, who has been introduced to our readers in the previous chapter, now appeared — the perspiration pouring off his brow; and, bending beneath the weight of a well-filled

---

* This treacherous act was perpetrated at the battle of Malvern Hill, as stated. Poor Willis, who inflicted such summary retribution, was afterwards killed.

knapsack,* he presented the appearance of one laboring under sore affliction.

"Well, me man o' wax," quoth Tim, " ye's looks tired an' purty well played out!"

"It's not exhausted, nayther is it debilitated, I am; nor is this perspiration exhumed from my flesh by the unaccustomed exercise of my fermoral muscles; but I am greatly exercised by the rapacious villany of a dishonest soger, whose audacious immorality has culminated in the appropriation of my frying-pan!"

Jimmie and Tim seemed stunned for a moment by the Professor's eloquence; the latter at last recovered himself, and said, "It must be a quare frying-pan; if yer plase, let's look at it."

"Haven't I explained to ye, in the clearest terrums, words, and expressions, that can be taken, picked, chosen, or selected from the unlimited vocabulary of the English tongue, the frying-pan that was attached to my back has taken unto itself wings and flown away!" and the Professor looked about him with as much dignity as his red, freckled face and extensive knapsack would allow.

---

* The author has observed that skulkers, stragglers, and army bummers carry the heaviest loads in clothes, kitchen utensils, and rations, and will not surrender them, even if dying with fatigue.

"O, it must be the divil's own frying-pan that could get off that way; it dropped off, ye mane."

"Ye war niver at Maynooth," interrupted the Professor, with a self-satisfied look.

"No," said Tim, innocently, "but I've a brother that was."

"Did he take his degrees?" queried the Professor.

"He did, indeed. I don't know what you call 'em, but he took something, and that's what got him there. Were you ever there?" asked Tim, in his turn.

"Faith, I was; 'twas there I got my larnin'."

"The divil!" quoth the astonished Tim; "ye ought to be ashamed to tell it, ye reprobate!"

"To tell it!" exclaimed the astonished Professor.

"Yes," yelled Tim, "ye got yer larnin' in Maynooth Jail, and ye'd be boastin' of it. It's little that my brother Dick would do the likes o' that, though he can make a brush or break a stone as clever as the next man, an' he didn't serve half as long as you."

The astounded Professor gave his knapsack a hitch, and fell to the rear, away from the boys, who laughed long and boisterously.

"Well, he's a man of wonderful larnin', Tim," quoth Jimmie.

"Ay," replied Tim; and he sang the following stanza in a clear and not unmusical voice: —

"He's a fine and mighty janius, full of larnin' and of wit,
   And can spake of other nations that are far beyant the say;
   He can talk in Greek or Latin, or elucidate Sanscrit.
   He's the gratest livin' scholar in the univarsitay."

"I wonder what made him 'list," said Jimmie, when his companion had unburdened himself of the above elegant lines.

"What made him inlist, is it? sure that's aisily answered. He larned everything that there was to be larned, 'cept sogerin'; so he jist come here to complate his accomplishments by larnin' how to make coffee, eat hard tack and pork, and sleep on the could, could ground; an' thin he'll go home wid a big diary an' a skin full of *rumatics*. That's the way wid these *ambitious* min, Jimmie; they'd go to the ould boy hisself for larnin'. It's well for us we are not janiuses, eh, Jimmie?"

"Yes, and for Uncle Sam too, Tim; for these janiuses is allus behind when there's any fightin' to be done; they doos be examinin' the *juology* of the rocks. I seed the Purfessor, the last time we'd a cut at the 'Johnnies,' behind a big pile, and I axed what he war doin', an' he sed he war 'juologizin' or some sort of gizin of the rocks!"

Thus the boys would travel on, relating anecdotes of their military experiences, and throwing off comical descriptions of character which kept their companions in a continual roar of laughter. Reaching Lovettsville late in the day, all soon were busy cooking their suppers, preparatory to sleep.

CHAPTER XXIV.

Rectorstown. — How to estimate Compliments. — Wapping Heights. — Warrenton. — The Landlord played out. — Beverley Ford. — Our Camp. — Arrival of Conscripts. — We march for Culpepper.

INTELLIGENCE reached us the next morning that the left of the rebel column was but a few miles in front; and at an early hour the regiment resumed its march, and after bivouacking three times, at Oatland's, and Goose Creek, arrived, on the evening of July 22, at Rectorstown, Va., through which, we learned, the victorious Mosby had passed the day before. We marched through this wretched place next day, and found it to contain a few wooden houses, several diminutive pigs, and a number of sharp, surly women, who, from their unladylike gestures and remarks, seemed to hold ourselves and flag in profound contempt; little notice was taken of them, however, though considerable attention was paid to the "grunters," many of which squealed their own most unmusical requiem. As we marched on, snuffing up the fresh air from the hills adjacent, and scanning the beautiful scenery by which this consumptive-looking town was surrounded, about noon, we arrived near Wapping Heights, a short distance from Manassas Gap.

Wapping Heights is a great rocky mountain, the Shenandoah Valley on one side, and the Manassas Station on the other. It is entirely devoid of vegetation, and the surface so sharp and pointed as to do great injury to the feet of the cavalry horses that passed over. At Wapping Heights we found the enemy drawn up in line of battle. Next day we attacked them, and they retreated in considerable confusion across the Shenandoah, having received a whipping from our forces.

We then turned our steps towards Warrenton, Virginia, and after two days' marching we halted and encamped about three miles from the town of Warrenton, which was a fine enterprising place before the war, and contained a population of two or three thousand inhabitants, among them many men of enterprise and ability. It contains several fine churches, and a number of public buildings, which, though now in a ruinous condition, still show traces of considerable architectural beauty. The streets are wide, well paved, and bordered by neatly-laid brick sidewalks; many beautiful lawns extend from the fronts of dwellings to the street, neatly enclosed by iron palisadings, and abutting on well-kept gardens. Several houses were surrounded with tastefully arranged flower beds, and here and there nice, comfortable-looking arbors and roomy porticos; just the place one could comfortably enjoy one's self of a summer evening with a friend, a book, or a cigar. This place looked more like the northern cities and towns than any other place we have visited south. We went to the large hotel there, but could not obtain anything. When we asked for wine, the eyes of the landlord nearly started from their sockets, as, in a flurried manner, he assured us that such an article he had not seen for over a year. "Nor whiskey?" we insinuated. "Nor whiskey," he answered, mournfully. So, at our suggestion, he showed us into a private room, where we produced our "private flask," at the sight of which he started back as though a Paixhan gun was aimed at him. We reassured him, however, and he took the flask and drank. He wiped his mouth with the back of his hand, and muttered, abstractedly, "Brandy."

"Ay," said we, turning to leave the hospitable mansion, "it's brandy." Whether that libation had any unfortunate effects upon the long abstemious landlord, we are not aware; but we left him in such a fit of astonishment at beholding the liquor that we were fearful he would never again recover the full use of his faculties.

From Warrenton the regiment marched to Beverley Ford, on the Rappahannock, where we encamped, about fifty yards from the river. The whole army was concentrated in the vicinity of the river, which in this place is about twenty yards wide.

Our camp at Beverley Ford was a very handsome one, and, seen from the surrounding elevations, presented quite a picturesque appearance. The streets, being laid out with due regard to comfort and the army regulations, were studded on either side with fir trees, which served as a protection from the sun, the weather being remarkably warm: being situate on a hill, it was very dry, and the men were soon able to make themselves comfortable. The distance to the picket lines was about half a mile, and the duty, therefore, far from irksome. We passed many pleasant days at Beverley Ford watching the rebels, and resting ourselves after the arduous marching we had undergone.

While here we were obliged to witness the public execution of five deserters from the One Hundred and Eighteenth Pennsylvania Regiment.[*] It was a strange and affecting scene, and was felt remarkably by our lads, many of whom said, at the time, they felt more cut up at this sight than at all the battles and battle-fields they had seen. We trust we shall never be called to witness such a sight again, though we fully maintain the justice of the sentence.

Shortly after this our regiment received a detachment of conscripted men and substitutes, the result of the first draft, from Long Island. We had heard a good deal of the draft, and were naturally anxious as to the kind of men we should get, as we found the commutation fee was taken advantage of by many who ought to have volunteered. Their arrival caused our camp to be very busy for a while, as they had to be drilled. Thus occupied, and with the kind of amusement incidental to our other camps, we passed away the time until the 15th of Septem-

---

[*] The same that so shamefully retreated at Boteler's Mills and Fredericksburg.

ber, when, with the rest of the army, we moved forward, crossing the river at Rappahannock Station. Our men had by this time become at home with their new associates, who would listen with interest to our fellows, as they related their adventures, and in return would detail their own.

CHAPTER XXV.

Culpepper. — Insinuating Females. — Picket Duty. — Drummed out. — Speculations. — Guerrillas. — " De ole Man's a grazing eber since." — A " What is it?" — A Negro Gymnast. — A crazy Professor. — Uncle Jolly and his good kind Sisters.

FROM the Rappahannock we moved forward, and marched through the town of Culpepper. Like the rest of the towns and cities of Virginia, Culpepper is greatly depopulated by the war, and from the fresh, bright, and cleanly appearance it seemed formerly to have presented, had merged into a dingy, dirty-looking place. When we saw it, its principal buildings, having been used as hospitals and barracks, were rapidly tumbling to pieces. The place boasted of many stores, the majority of which were closed; and we noticed some very handsome private dwellings. When we arrived, the sutlers who had preceded us were driving a very profitable traffic in disposing of preserved fruits, meat, and vegetables, tobacco and cigars, soda and other articles comparatively useless to the soldier, but done up in such tempting packages that it was nearly impossible to resist the purchase.

The female portion of the inhabitants watched our progress with some interest, but did not scruple to inform us that we should soon leave with the redoubtable "rebs" behind us. We marched along, however, intending to stop as long as necessary, and to leave only when General Meade should order us; and we felt in no wise hurt at the covert insinuations of these thoughtless ladies. When we had marched some two miles outside the town we halted in a small wood on the south side of the main road, and there pitched our camp. Being so close to the depot, supplies were plentiful; and therefore many important messing elements were at our command. One great luxury to the soldier was here in abundance — "soft bread." This was brought by rail from Washington, was very often supplied, and, after having been confined to "hard tack," the change was most welcome.

Our regiment here, with others, performed picket duty, and passed the time away very comfortably.

One day, while here, they were treated to the

exhibition of a deserter being drummed out, which was looked upon as a good joke by our boys. The culprit, a poor half-witted looking fellow, after being marched in front of all the brigade, had the hair cut off one side of his head, quite close, making him look like a mountebank; then, being branded with the letter D, with a great deal of drumming of the tune known as the "Rogue's March," he was allowed to go on his way. Beyond this nothing of interest transpired at this camp out of the ordinary routine of military life. We strolled about the fields, patronized the "settlers" to the extent of our currency, smoked their abominably bad cigars, and visited, as often as circumstances would allow, the commissary of our brigade, who, in certain matters, was nearly omnipotent. We entertained our friends, and they entertained us, both parties ventilating old and new stories, and, when not employed in this way, anathematizing the weather, or speculating on the kind of reception we should meet *when* we arrived at Richmond. We paid an attentive ear to the news from the North; and when the "draft was commenced," we fervently wished we were at home to help enforce it. When we learned of the disgraceful New York riots, how heartily we wished for a chance to give those fellows a taste of our quality, and show them how the Irish Ninth could charge; but, as none of these gratifying duties were vouchsafed us, we would drop the discussion of the subject with maledictions on the copperheads, who were considered infinitely more contemptible than the crawling viper — the thing from which they have received their name.

The guerrillas, hovering about the flanks of our army, would sometimes cause a little excitement, by gobbling up quartermasters and staff officers, or seizing ambulances containing our sick and wounded; but these little ventures were speedily stopped by our cavalry, who were now in a fine state of discipline, and exhibiting more dash every day.

One day, while here, we came upon a negro family, who were living near what had once been almost a palatial mansion; the cabin was of log, the interstices being filled with clay, covered with a roof of thatch, browned by the action of the atmosphere. A broken rail fence, which enclosed the hut, and a dilapidated pigsty, within which four young "grunters" and their maternal "parient" were industriously rooting up the mud, comprised the limited domain of the venerable darky who was the presiding genius. We engaged him in conversation, who was nothing loath to converse with any one, leaning on his stick, apparently about eighty years of age, bent nearly double. As he stood beside his hut, we asked him, after a while, if he was a slave. He said, "No, dey kep de ole man as long as dere was any good in him, and worked him like a beast; and now they've turned him out to graze, and de ole man's a-grazing eber since."

There was much pathos in the mournful tone of the old man as he said this, and he shook his head and moved slowly away. We thought, as we stood musing, what a terrible thing to have to pass eighty long years in slavery; and, when the sap and vigor of manhood's usefulness had been wrung from him, like the withered trunk of the once stalwart tree, become useless, then, and only *then*, in the expressive words of the poor old darky, to be turned out, like a broken-down horse, "to graze" and die. Such was the idea that crossed our crude, free, northern mind, and we felt, more than ever, in heart and principle, an uncompromising enmity to human slavery.

Of this family was one of the queerest specimens of negro boys we ever saw. He was slimly built, from ten to twelve years old, with a huge misshapen head loosely set on his shoulders, and a countenance of the drollest description it is possible to conceive. As we first saw him, he was partly concealed by some logs of timber, with his head thrust forward, and his large eyes rolling at us with a peculiar expression of drollery. One of "ours" seized him by the scalp and drew him forth from his hiding-place; he stood for a moment on his feet, and then bounded away on all fours, with uncommon rapidity. On reaching the foot of a large tree, he scrambled up with the agility of a monkey, and ran out far on a branch at a dizzy height above us, and sat there, seeming to enjoy our amazement. After a little while, he came down; at a bound leaped upon the back of our horse; but, before we could catch him, he was gone, and had cleared the fence, and was out of sight. The next time we saw him he was perched upon the branch of a tree, squatting upon his haunches, eating some corn-cake, which he dexterously extracted from his pocket while in that position. When he came down, he remained seated at the bottom for a moment, and then, with an extraordinary effort, sprang from the ground, and clutching a branch more than twelve feet above him, adroitly swung himself up into the tree. When we saw the old man, we said, —

"That's a smart boy of yours."

"Smart? yes, he's smart! too smart! too smart!" was the old man's reply, at the same time directing our attention to a heap of some ten or twelve corn cobs which the youngster had just polished off for his lunch, not exactly to the old man's satisfaction. We stuck a greenback high up on a pine, close by, for the boy, and rode away. On looking round, ere we had gone far, to our surprise he was upon our horse's haunches, examining the note attentively; upon seeing our astonished look, he sprang to the ground and bounded away. Many of the officers saw much more of his gymnastic feats, and expressed their astonishment at the drollery of his antics. That boy reminded us very much of Barnum's "What is it," only he was "more so."

We turned our horse's head in the direction of a large slate-colored house, about a quarter of a mile distant. Arriving there, we asked a colored man we met at the gate, if we could get a drink of milk. "Yas," he answered; and, opening the gate, we passed in. Going up the gravel pathway, we came upon a fine-looking, stout old gentleman, who bowed to us with the stately courtesy of the old school. Learning our wishes, he preceded us to a wing of the mansion, and, putting his face to an open window, shouted, "Sally, milk for the gentleman." In a moment, Sally — a very comely-looking young colored woman — appeared with the milk, which we took and drank, and were about to return the mug, when, behind the pleasant face of Sally, at the open window, we saw the faces of three ladies, who seemed to gaze upon us with much complacency, — or else 'twas our conceit that led us to think so. We bowed politely, when the old gentleman bawled out, "My sisters, sir! my sisters!" Again we bowed, somewhat astonished at the gruffness of the old gentleman. The ladies asked us to dismount — a request we were not slow in obeying; for a vision of warm rolls, bright yellow butter, and new milk, passed before us, completely eclipsing the frugal fare of camp. The old gentleman seemed highly pleased when we dismounted, and, rubbing his hands gleefully, ushered us into a neat, cool, and comfortable parlor, tastefully arranged. We found the ladies very well informed, and, without flattery, very pretty — we won't say beautiful. They seemed to regard the old gentleman with peculiar affection, intermingled with considerable anxiety, the reason of which for some time we could not ascertain. After some conversation, he introduced the subject of the present rebellion. We had always made it a point never to discuss the subject with a rebel, or resident in any evacuated country; and in this case scarcely replied to him, making every possible effort to divert the conversation into some other channel; happening, unwittingly, to quote a line from Shakspeare, the old gentleman started from his seat, throwing back the scanty hair from his forehead, and assuming an erect, defiant attitude, began, —

"Either thou wilt die, by God's just ordinance,
Ere from this war thou turn a conqueror,
Or I with grief and extreme age shall perish,
And never look upon thy face again.
Therefore, take with thee my most heavy curse,
Which, in the day of battle, tire thee more
Than all the complete armor that thou wearest!
My prayers on the adverse party fight;
And then the little souls of Edward's children
Whip the spirit of their enemies,

> And promise them success and victory.
> Bloody thou art, bloody will be thy end;
> Shame serves thy life, and will thy death attend!"

We gazed at him with astonishment, nor could scarcely understand the meaning of his declamation. Finally, having run through a variety of quotations from Richard, he paused; his eyes filled with a strange light, and, wiping his brow with his handkerchief, he sat down and looked towards us as though awaiting our approval. Scarcely knowing what to do, we turned to the ladies. One of them made a scarcely perceptible motion, and moved from the room. In a few moments we followed, and from her we learned that the old gentleman was demented. He was formerly a professor in a college in Virginia, and possessed extraordinary abilities; but by over-application, his mind gave way, and now he was only fit —

> "For sweet seclusion . . .
> For calm, uninterrupted solitude."

All this we learned with solemn surprise, and turning, beheld the unfortunate subject of our conversation standing at the parlor door, gazing at us with an expression of distrust and suspicion. He was a most noble-looking man, with a brow broad, thoughtful, and indicative of the fine intellect which now lay dormant within. He was in the habit of strolling around the neighborhood, being known as Uncle Jollie, and was freed from any annoyance in consequence. We staid to tea; and when we took our departure, left the poor gentleman greatly grieved and disappointed, as we had become great friends. He shook hands with us, and begged that we would visit him again. To this we assented, if convenient, and came away. Though circumstances have prevented our repeating the visit, yet we shall look back with pleasure to the pleasant evening spent with this family, and feel grateful for the kind attention shown us by those ladies — a course so unusual with the fair sex of Virginia.

CHAPTER XXVI.

Rainy Weather. — Damp Meditations. — The Rapidan before. — The Rappahannock behind. — Counter Strategy. — Bull Run. — The old Battle-ground. — The Death of Kearney. — Graves of the gallant Dead. — The dead Sentinel. — Heroic Mementos. — March to Gainesville. — Army Wagons rolling over the Dead.

RAINY weather came upon us. O the *ennui* of those days! We sat within the tents, the flaps thrown back, gazing out upon the falling water, and the miniature rivers cutting their irregular way through the soft yellow soil and rushing along the drains of the camp, and forming themselves into great pools, and looking as if the tide of the mighty deluge was fast receding, and earth in her native modesty peeping out for sunshine's smile.

The trees seemed to droop and weep; and the little dirty brown tents looked as if heartily ashamed of their cramped, uncomfortable, and very " unjolly " appearance; the fires would struggle fitfully for a moment to warm the damp hands and dry the saturated garments of their uncomfortable guests, and then flicker down under the torrent in a mass of thick blue smoke, through which a little tongue of flame would sometimes flit to show

"That still she lived."

You could hear, too, the unweary axe, with its monotonous chop, chop, from the woods, and the voice of the woodman soldier, as he plied his toil, singing merrily in the rain. This dismal weather did not long continue, however, and when the rain ceased, and the sun came out, we issued from our canvas huts, stretched our unexercised anatomy, and prepared to move. We fell back from the Rapidan, passed through Culpepper, much to the *delight* of its inhabitants, marched to the Rappahannock, which we crossed the same day, and moved to Warrenton Junction, where General Meade concentrated the army of the Potomac, and prepared to oppose by counter-strategy the strategic movements of Lee. In this General Meade was eminently successful. In the progress of his movements he arrived at Beverley Ford, where he expected Lee would give battle. A few days after, the battle of Bristow Station was fought, about the 14th of October, in which the

Second Corps acted with splendid gallantry, having been cut off from the main army, and succeeded in repulsing the enemy. About midnight of the day of the battle of Bristow Station, the Fifth Corps came to their assistance. The Ninth endured great fatigue during that day and night, having marched from Bristow Station to Centreville, and back to Fairfax, where they encamped for the night. The next day we marched to the old *Battle-Ground of Bull Run,* where we arrived October 20, 1863. The battle-ground is a series of low hills, intersected with narrow streams of good water, the great essential of a battle-field or camp-ground.

The fiercest part of the contest under Pope was fought in broad, open fields fenced in along the north-east side, with dense woods, at that time occupied by our cavalry, which, supported by the Pennsylvania reserves, made a most splendid charge upon the forces of the enemy, over the open field, fences, and streams, upon the rebels in position at that point, driving them to the shelter of the wood upon the south-west portion of the field.

The contest in the open field must have been very fierce, for piles of dead are accumulated upon every part of this memorable ground; and wherever one walks perfect skeletons present themselves to the eye, some still clad in uniform, and others, in a crumbled state of fallen glory, still retain vestiges of the livery in which they fought and died. They are principally the skeletons of Southern soldiers, who, in charging across the plain, fell in hundreds, under the fierce fire that flashed from the guns of our gallant men.*

The field of Bull Run is the most memorable in the history of the war for the desperate valor of the combatants, and the tenacity with which, for a whole day, the ground upon which they fought was contested; for the gallant men who fell there; for the blow which for a time retarded our progress upon the Confederate capital. We rode to the spot at Chantilly, upon the west side, from out of which Kearney advanced to reconnoitre the enemy's position, and where he received the fatal wound which cut him off in the zenith of his glory.

The Ninth was encamped upon one of the hills referred to, and for hundreds of yards graves ran out in every direction. Deep hollows pointed out the spot where the dead men lay sleeping

---

* 1863.

in their glory. The ground had fallen in over the fleshless forms and bleaching skulls, and rough pieces of board were the unwritten obituaries of the gallant fallen, who had stemmed the tide of battle up to that spot where they made their last stand, and sighed out their last breath for their country!

A few horses were scattered among the hills, shattered by the shot and shell of the contending forces, dumb witnesses of the struggle in which they had occupied so distinguished a part.

We rode into the woods which circled the place, for the purpose of watering our horse. The moon glimmered down through the interstices of the trees, and the wind sighed gently among the branches, and off on the hills the camp fires of the soldiers burned while the gallant, weary fellows profoundly slept beside them.

We dismounted and led our horse to a spring that bubbled up in the moonlight. He darted aside in affright. We looked to ascertain the cause of his fear, and beheld, in a sitting attitude, with his back to a tree, the form of a man. He was so silent and motionless that we approached, after vainly calling to him, and placed our hands upon his shoulder; they rested there heavily for a second; we shook him, and the form crumbled to dust under our touch.

It was the skeleton of a Southern cavalryman, in full dress, who had, doubtless, crawled there to assuage his thirst, and, exhausted, had leaned against the tree, with his dying eyes upon the rich, cool, crystal stream that ran murmuring at his feet, which, in his helpless, dying agony, he had been unable to reach! Alone in death he had sentinelled that stream, the dead faithfully performing the duties of the good soldier, until from a stranger's touch he assimilated with the dust from which he sprung!

The country, for miles about Bull Run, is undulating in character, covered with brush, and crossed by streams in many places. A few ruined houses still are standing, riddled with ball and shell, indexes of the fierce nature of the artillery fire during that memorable fight. Cartridge boxes, bayonet scabbards, and gun stocks are strewn in every direction, fallen from the nerveless hands of wounded men, or lying complete upon the skeletons of the dead. One could scarcely contemplate the scene without feelings of sadness, mingled with pride, at the glorious valor of our people, and the reckless heroism they ever display in defence of whatever cause or principle they may espouse.

As we moved along the road to Gainesville on the afternoon of October 20, 1863, we beheld innumerable graves by the road-side — a few hasty shovels of dirt cast upon the poor fellows on the spot where they had fearlessly fallen. Skulls and member bones of human forms, cracked under the wheels of army wagons, eliciting no other remark than, "There's more of them yonder," or, "They fell thick and fast here"—language seemingly cold and unsympathetic, but uttered in a tone which told how keenly they pitied the poor, neglected bones that once formed the good husband, the noble son, the brave brother, the gallant, impulsive, patriot soldier! That portion of Virginia is one immense cemetery — one vast graveyard, daily ploughed by never-ending lines of army wagons. It is vaster than Waterloo—more grand and startling in the fierce heroism of its reminiscences.

CHAPTER XXVII.

A Rebel Camp. — Rebel Sufferings and Rebel Sympathizers. — Condition of Rebel Camps. — Of Union Camps. — Preserve us from the Attributes of Southern Chivalry. — New Baltimore. — Auburn. — Three-mile Station. — Rappahannock Station. — Storming the Enemy's Works. — Brandy Station.— General Meade and his Movements. — The Ninth in the Position of Honor and Danger. — The Invitation to Death. — Description of Mine Run. — Winter Quarters. — Bealton.

ABOUT three miles from Bull Run is erected quite a village of substantial log-houses, capable of holding from ten to twenty men each. They were built by the rebels and used as winter quarters after the close of the first campaign. They must have lived very comfortably at that time, while our troops only *enjoyed* the shelter of the "ponchos." Much of the suffering afterwards said to have been undergone by the rebels only existed in the imagination of their sympathizers. In all things, with, perhaps, the single exception of food, they were quite comfortable.

We are convinced of this from the fact that

their evacuated camps and the general appearance of those who have fallen into our hands have conclusively proved it. A rebel camp is generally filthy and ill kept, its sanitary condition seeming to be a matter of little or no consequence. Comfort, so far as protection from wind, rain, and cold was concerned, is to the rebel the most important preliminary to the pitching of a camp. Drainage and sinks are accommodations scarcely known, or, if known, rarely used by them. When they halt, they occupy the ground with all its attendant evils and accumulated filth, and when they break camp for the march, the only difference in the condition of the place is that it is more loathsome and filthy than before. The Northern soldier, on the contrary, is a model of order and cleanliness, and no finer camps were ever pitched in active service, in modern or ancient times, than those of our troops at Miner's Hill, on the peninsula, or at Beverley Ford. Cleanliness, regularity, and *refined* discipline are noticeable attributes in the sturdy Northerner of America. And if this distinguished peculiarity is proof of blood and breeding inferior to the *pseudo* "chivalry" of the South, let us accept the token of inferiority, and be unto the Giver of all things devoutly thankful.

From Bull Run the army moved towards New Baltimore, a village containing a few houses, but at that time scarcely any inhabitants. We finally encamped at a place called Auburn, and the following morning continued our march in the direction of Three-mile Station, where we again encamped only to move the next morning to Rappahannock Station, where we soon engaged in a most interesting battle.

The works at that place extended along the line of the Rappahannock for a number of miles, and were considered by military critics to be very formidable. It was decided to storm the works. During the night, the regiments selected to perform the labor crept, under cover of the darkness, to within one hundred and fifty yards of them, and after an hour's patient waiting, they advanced, and charged rapidly down upon the shadowy earth-line, bristling with the muzzles of innumerable guns. With such vigor, silence, and courage was the charge made as scarcely to allow of resistance. An incoherent and disconnected volley of small arms from the enemy — a desultory roar from a few cannon —

and the works were ours. In fact, the change of ownership was so rapidly effected as scarcely to be realized by the rebels, who fled in great confusion to the river, in which many were drowned, and on the banks of which numbers were captured or killed.

General Meade rapidly effected the passage of his army over the different fords, the Fifth Army Corps moving towards Brandy Station, where the Ninth took possession of the winter quarters of the rebels — log-houses well built in the woods, which, on account of uncleanliness, as usual, we demolished, simply pitching our shelter-tents, which, if not so comfortable, were at least clean, military, and wholesome. Here we remained until the morning of November 26, 1863, when General Meade made his memorable movement on Lee, in fortified position near Orange Court House, in the County of Orange, Va., and but a few miles distant from Chancellorsville, the scene of General Hooker's three days' movement, and from which he effected his remarkable retreat a few months before.

Two great and unsuccessful movements have been made on this ground, the army under Meade pushing deepest into the enemy's country. The movement of General Meade seemed to be characterized by great caution, which was certainly needful, for he was in a dangerous territory. The Ninth Regiment occupied no unimportant part in this series of great movements which finally terminated in the great game of "blind man's buff" at Mine Run. The Ninth was placed in one of the foremost and most distinguished positions at Mine Run, being called upon, in conjunction with the remainder of the brigade, by a special order, to be prepared to storm, at a stated hour, one of the most impregnable and important rebel positions they ever faced during their thirty months of marches and battles. The Ninth Regiment on the right of the Fifth Corps, the position of honor and danger, and close to the river or "run," which was a main defence of the contending force, would be among the first precipitated into the battle. For a long time after the order had been read to them, they awaited with eagerness and impatience that invitation to death, uttered in the single word "forward!" and truly, if ever men longed for battle, they did; for they were actually freezing as they lay inactive on the ground, and many did die from cold ere they left that most *blessed* and impregnable position. To fully appreciate the uncomfortable danger of the duty they were to perform, the reader must remember that in charging, the Ninth must pass through the freezing waters of Mine Run, a stream of perhaps ten feet in width, very shallow, if we may judge by the depth of clear water, but very deep when we count in the mud at its bottom. At its sides, extending several rods back, is a low marsh, miry and reed-grown. From the edges of the marsh the land rises gradually to a height of perhaps a hundred feet. A half mile back from either shore these slopes are open, and in many places cultivated patches of young pines dot the slopes, and extend back to the dense woods which crown the summits of the hills. The run rises somewhere south of the old plank road, and flows lazily northward to the river, in nearly a straight line. The enemy had fortified the west slope by a strong earthwork at its summit, in front of which felled trees, and shrubbery, and brush formed an impenetrable abatis; they had also dug a succession of pits half way up the slope, within easy musket range of the creek, and another series of the same style of defences at the commencement of the abatis. His line of defences extended from Clark's Mountain, south of the plank road, to the mouth of the stream, and was fully supported by artillery, and was, in fact, said by military men to be a stronger position than he held at Fredericksburg.

"Our own artillery was planted upon the side of the eastern slope, a few rods down from the edge of the timber, while our infantry was covered from view by the thick wood. In order to successfully operate upon the enemy with infantry, it became necessary to bridge the stream and morass in several places — a work you will imagine to be both difficult and dangerous. It was done, however, by the first divisions of the First and Third Corps respectively. Darkness found us, on Sunday night, in the following position: The Second Corps was on the extreme left in the vicinity of Clark's Mountain, reënforced by one division of the Sixth Corps. The left centre was held by the Third Corps; the centre by two divisions of the First, and the right by the Fifth and the remaining two divisions of the Sixth Corps. General Warren was to have attacked and turned the enemy's right wing at three o'clock in the afternoon. The Fifth and Sixth, under Sykes and Sedgwick, were, at the same time, to attack his left, while the Third and First were to make a demonstration upon his centre. The reserves of artillery had all been brought forward and positioned ready for action; but for some reason General Warren failed to connect, and night slipped in upon us, all drawn up in line of battle. That night a change was made in the programme. General Warren did not deem his force adequate to the task of turning the enemy's right; so he was still further re-enforced by two divisions of the Third Corps, under Generals Carr and Prince, while Birney, with his division of the same corps, was to support the artillery.

Eight o'clock on Monday morning was then set as the hour for the great battle to open, and we retired to our ground-beds to rest and dream. The night of Sunday was the coldest we had yet experienced. Ice formed in the streams an inch in thickness, and several of the men froze their limbs, and one or two their lives out, while doing duty as pickets. At eight o'clock on Monday, the artillery began to play upon the enemy, and for an hour, I think, the firing was as constant and heavy as I ever witnessed; but the infantry did not make any demonstrations whatever; and, after a deal of noise and the waste of a large amount of ammunition, the artillery was silenced by an order from general headquarters, which brought us back unmolested, but sore and weary, to our old camping-grounds.

From our old camp at Brandy Station, we continued our march until we reached the Rappahannock, where rumors were rife that the campaign was ended, and the army going into winter quarters. This, the reader will believe, was welcome intelligence to us all, after our weeks of marching, freezing, and fighting. Our depleted columns surely needed reënforcing, and our exhausted soldiers were in great need of rest; so, when we crossed the Rappahannock, and learned that the Second Brigade, First Division, Fifth Corps, army of the Potomac, was to be detached from the army and sent to Bealton Station, to guard the line of railroad at that place, we felt satisfied that the campaign was over, and that the wished-for period of rest was at hand.

We resumed our march, and, towards evening, reached Bealton, and finally encamped in a beautiful pine wood, near to the railroad, where, in a few days, log-huts were erected, and the Ninth engaged in completing their winter quarters.

CHAPTER XXVIII.

Bealton Station. — Winter Duties. — Mosby's Guerrillas. — Black Horse Cavalry. — Cutting Railroads. — Vigilance and Valor. — A March. — The coming Wilderness. — The Battle of the Wilderness. — Irish Heroism. — Spottsylvania. — Bethesda Church. — Shady Oak. — Cold Harbor. — The Dead. — Home and Muster-out.

THE Ninth remained encamped at Bealton Station until the 30th day of April, 1864,[*] guarding that portion of the Alexandria and Orange Railroad lying between Licking Run and Bealton, and also picketing a portion of the line from Freedman's Ford, on the Rappahannock, to Warrenton Junction.

The duties performed during these winter months were very arduous, and required the greatest vigilance, in consequence of the frequent raids of Mosby's guerrillas, and also of the notorious company of "Black Horse Cavalry." The latter force consisted principally of the

---

[*] From Major J. W. Mahan's record in Adjutant-General's Reports.

flower of Fauquier County, and was the first company of cavalry mustered into the service of the Confederate States. It took its name from the fact that its first captain rode a splendid black charger; and the company was always known, even prior to the war, as the Black Horse Cavalry, and formed part of the Virginia militia.

Several attempts to cut the railroad and burn the bridge at Licking Run were foiled by the vigilance and valor of the Ninth Regiment, and its services were appreciated by the division commander in an appropriate order.

On the 30th of April, early in the morning, the Ninth broke camp, and at night bivouacked near Freedman's Ford. On the morning of the 1st of May, the regiment crossed to the south side of the Rappahannock, and encamped near Brandy Station. From thence they marched to Culpepper; and on the morning of the 4th, shortly after daybreak, our weary veterans crossed the Rapidan, without opposition, and bivouacked the same night in the ever-memorable Wilderness.

Here we would fain rest our pen, leaving others to write the sad, but glorious remainder of our story — to tell the sacrifice of our young braves, the true and trusty, who dashed into battle in the light of our stars, and with visions of home before them, fell in the front in victory!

But history, which is not written for to-day, but for all time, does not allow the exercise of useless regrets or vain sorrowings. It demands a consistent following of the record, even if, to pen it, the wounds reopen, and the old sorrows return afresh.

On the morning of May 5, the enemy was reported moving on our lines, and the line of battle was formed, breastworks of logs were thrown up, and about one o'clock in the afternoon heavy skirmishing commenced. Shortly after, the regiment was ordered to leave the works and support the first line, then advancing to charge the enemy's position. The advance was through a dense wood, from which the enemy was driven into a small plain. Beyond this plain was another piece of woods, where the enemy was found to be intrenched. In the advance the gallant conduct of the Ninth Regiment was splendidly apparent. The officers, cool and fearless, fell fast, cheering their men on in their heroic work, careless of life and only wishing for a victory. Upon reaching the plain, the enemy were found to be in possession of a section of artillery; and Lieutenant-Colonel Hanley, then commanding the regiment, in the absence of Colonel Guiney, — who, terribly wounded by a minie ball in the left eye, which was totally destroyed, had been carried to the rear, — ordered a charge to recover possession of it; and for some time the conflict raged desperately. But the enemy were finally driven to their works, from which they poured a most destructive fire of musketry on our still advancing line.

By some mistake of orders, the regiment on our right did not move to our support; and being thus exposed to a flank fire, Lieutenant-Colonel Hanley ordered the regiment to fall back to the edge of the woods, which was done in good order, and the line re-formed. The enemy again advanced to repossess themselves of the plain, but they were once more driven to seek the shelter of their works, and the disputed ground was held by the regiment until orders came from General Griffin to fall back to the line of breastworks. The fierce battles of the 6th and 7th of May followed, and the Ninth regiment, with its usual fortune, was constantly in the front line; but the nature of the ground was better, affording more protection, and the loss was, consequently, slight.

On the 8th day of May, after marching all night, and without halting to partake of food, the regiment opened the battle of Laurel Hill, which lasted from twelve o'clock (noon) until dark, resulting in a substantial victory, as the enemy were driven a mile and a half, and the coming of night alone prevented their complete defeat.

The final efforts of our noble regiment at Spottsylvania, the Rivers Po and North Anna, Bethesda Church, Shady Oak, and Cold Harbor, sustained its past reputation for valor and fidelity to the cause of the Union, and completed a record of Irish martial valor worthy of a people who in every age were distinguished for their warlike attributes.

The following named officers fell in that fierce and decisive campaign:—

JAMES W. MACNAMARA, Captain.
WILLIAM A. PHELAN, "
NICHOLAS C. FLAHERTY, Lieutenant.
JAMES O'NEILL, "
ARCHIBALD SIMPSON, "
CHARLES B. McGINNISKIN, "

These are the names of the gallant men chosen to attest, by their valor, the devotion of their regiment to the cause of freedom and the proud emblem they ever gallantly and gloriously upheld.

Their best monument is the commemoration of history. In going to death they bravely aided in delivering a race from bondage.

HOME AND MUSTER-OUT.

On the 10th day of June, 1864, the term of service of the Ninth Regiment having expired, it broke camp at daylight, and marched from Bottom Bridge, where the regiment had been under heavy fire, to White House Landing, on the Pamunkey River, and on the 11th took transports for Washington, where it arrived Sunday, June 12. June 13, the Ninth took cars for New York, in which city the regiment encamped on the 14th. At Baltimore, Philadelphia, and New York we were received with the greatest kindness, and collations served, and other hospitalities tendered.

On the morning of the 15th day of June, we

arrived at Boston, and met a cordial and hearty reception. If the citizens who so generously received and entertained us experienced joy at the return of their regiment, it would be scarcely more than a tithe of the feelings of gratitude which the soldiers of the Irish Ninth felt for the noble honors which were done them, after the many glorious campaigns through which they had passed.

A company of the State militia formed the escort, and twenty-three civic associations joined in the procession. All the public buildings, and many private dwellings and stores, displayed the national colors, and were gayly decorated with bunting. A salute was fired on Boston Common, by Captain Cummings' Battery of light artillery, and at Faneuil Hall a splendid collation was served by the city of Boston. In the afternoon and evening the regiment was entertained in a becoming manner by the generous and patriotic members of the Columbian Association, and on the 21st day of June was mustered out of the service of the United States.

Thus the military history of the Irish Ninth was ended; its reception a fit conclusion to a glorious military career.

APPENDIX.

ROSTER OF THE OFFICERS

OF THE

NINTH REGIMENT MASS. VOL. INFANTRY.

THOMAS CASS, Colonel, was the principal organizer of the regiment; commissioned June 11, 1861; mortally wounded at the Battle of Malvern Hill, Va., July 1, 1862; died of wounds at his residence in Boston, July 12, 1862; buried at Mount Auburn Cemetery, Cambridge, with military honors.

PATRICK R. GUINEY, Colonel, assisted in recruiting and organizing the regiment; commissioned Captain, June 11, 1861; promoted Major, October 24, 1862; promoted Lieutenant-Colonel, July 28, 1862; complimented, in special orders, for bravery at the Battle of Gaines' Mills, June 27, 1862; promoted Colonel, July 26, 1862, for bravery on the field; lost left eye by a wound received at the Battle of the Wilderness, Va., May 5, 1864; mustered out with the regiment; promoted Brevet Brigadier-General, March 13, 1865, for gallant and meritorious services during the war; residence, Roxbury.

C. G. ROWELL, Lieutenant-Colonel, assisted in recruiting and organizing the regiment; commissioned June 11, 1861; resigned October 23, 1861; residence, Boston.

ROBERT PEARD, Lieutenant-Colonel, assisted in recruiting and organizing the regiment; commissioned Major, June 11, 1861;

promoted Lieutenant-Colonel, October 24, 1861; died of disease at Miner's Hill, Va., January 27, 1862; residence, Milford.

PATRICK T. HANLEY, Lieutenant-Colonel, assisted in recruiting and organizing the regiment; commissioned First Lieutenant, June 11, 1861; promoted Captain, August 26, 1861; promoted Major, January 28, 1862; promoted Lieutenant-Colonel, July 26, 1862, for bravery on the field; wounded at the Battle of Malvern Hill, Va., July 1, 1862; complimented in special orders for bravery during the Battle of Gaines' Mills, June 27, 1862; mustered out with the regiment; residence, Boston.

GEORGE W. DUTTON, Major, assisted in recruiting and organizing the regiment; commissioned Captain, June 11, 1861; promoted Major, August 26, 1862; wounded at the Battle of Malvern Hill, Va.; resigned at Falmouth, Va., on account of disability received from wounds, March 29, 1863; residence, Stoughton.

JOHN W. MAHAN, Major, assisted in recruiting and organizing the regiment; commissioned First Lieutenant, June 11, 1861; promoted Captain, October 25, 1861; promoted Major, March 30, 1863; mustered out with the regiment; residence, Boston.

PETER PINEO, Surgeon, commissioned June 11, 1861; appointed Brigade Inspector; promoted Medical Inspector, Army of the Potomac, with the rank of Lieutenant-Colonel, August 27, 1861; residence, Boston.

STEPHEN W. DREW, Surgeon, commissioned August 27, 1861; resigned December 6, 1862, at Falmouth, Va.; residence, Woburn.

JAMES T. SULLIVAN, Surgeon, commissioned Assistant Surgeon, July 31, 1862; promoted Surgeon, December 13, 1862; mustered out with the regiment; residence, Chelsea.

PATRICK A. O'CONNELL, Assistant Surgeon, commissioned June 11, 1861; resigned September 12, 1861; afterwards Medical Director of the Ninth Army Corps; residence, Boston.

FRANCIS M. LINCOLN, Assistant Surgeon, commissioned September 12, 1861; promoted Surgeon 35th Mass. Vols., July 28, 1862; residence, Boston.

JAMES W. FITZPATRICK, Assistant Surgeon, commissioned August 14, 1862; promoted Surgeon of Volunteers, March 29, 1863; residence, Boston.

JOHN RYAN, Assistant Surgeon, commissioned December 13, 1862; mustered out with the regiment; residence, Boston.

ROSTER OF THE OFFICERS. 251

THOMAS SCULLY, Chaplain, commissioned June 17, 1861; resigned on account of ill health, October 31, 1862; residence, Boston.

CHARLES L. EGAN, Chaplain, commissioned September 18, 1863; mustered out with the regiment; afterwards commissioned by the War Department Hospital Chaplain, and remained on Brevet Major-General Charles Griffin's (5th A. C.) staff till the close of the rebellion; residence, Washington, D. C.

GEORGE W. PERKINS, Adjutant, assisted in recruiting and organizing the regiment; commissioned First Lieutenant and Adjutant, June 11, 1861; resigned August 4, 1861; residence, Boston.

WILLIAM STRACHAN, Adjutant, enlisted as Sergeant Major, June 11, 1861; promoted First Lieutenant and Adjutant, August 26, 1861; cashiered February 25, 1862; afterwards reënlisted as private, August 14, 1862; recommended for re-commission, but the numerical strength of the regiment would not admit of any more promotions; discharged at Falmouth, Va.; residence, Boston.

JOHN M. TOBIN, Adjutant, assisted in recruiting and organizing the regiment; commissioned First Lieutenant, June 11, 1861; appointed Adjutant, February 25, 1862; promoted Captain, August 28, 1862; wounded at the Battle of the Wilderness, Va., May 5, 1864; mustered out with the regiment; residence, Boston.

MICHAEL W. PHALEN, Adjutant, enlisted as First Sergeant of Company F, June 11, 1861; promoted Second Lieutenant, September 7, 1861; promoted First Lieutenant, January 28, 1862; appointed Adjutant, August 28, 1862; wounded at the Battles of Gaines' Mills and Mine Run, Va.; mustered out with the regiment; residence, Salem.

JOHN MORAN, Quartermaster, commissioned First Lieutenant and Quartermaster, June 11, 1861; resigned November 26, 1861; residence, Boston.

THOMAS MOONEY, Quartermaster, enlisted as Quartermaster Sergeant, June 11, 1861; promoted First Lieutenant and Quartermaster, November 27, 1861; thrown from his horse, and fatally injured, March 17, 1863, at Falmouth, Va.; died from the injuries received, March 26, 1863, at Washington, D. C.

DANIEL G. MACNAMARA, Quartermaster, assisted in recruiting and organizing the regiment; enlisted as First Sergeant of Company E, June 11, 1861; promoted Commissary Sergeant, March 10, 1862; promoted Second Lieutenant, September 26, 1862; promoted First Lieutenant, August 27, 1862, to rank from date of commission; appointed Quartermaster at Falmouth, Va., March 26, 1863; mustered out with the regiment; residence, Boston.

JAMES E. GALLAGHER, Captain, assisted in recruiting and organizing the regiment; commissioned June 11, 1861; resigned July 9, 1862; residence, Boston.

CHRISTOPHER PLUNKETT, Captain, assisted in recruiting and organizing the regiment; commissioned Captain, June 11, 1861; resigned August 7, 1861; reënlisted as a private, August 14, 1862; promoted Second Lieutenant, September 26, 1862; promoted First Lieutenant, January 8, 1863; wounded — right arm carried away by a twelve-pound solid shot — at the Battle of the North Anna, May 23, 1864; mustered out with the regiment; residence, Boston.

WILLIAM MADIGAN, Captain, assisted in recruiting and organizing the regiment; commissioned Captain, June 11, 1861; killed in action at the Battle of Gaines' Mills, Va., June 27, 1862.

JOHN R. TEAGUE, Captain, commissioned Captain, June 11, 1861; resigned January 27, 1862; residence, Boston.

EDWARD FITZGERALD, Captain, assisted in recruiting and organizing the regiment; commissioned Captain, June 11, 1861; resigned September 3, 1861; residence, Salem.

JOHN CAREY, Captain, assisted in recruiting and organizing the regiment; commissioned Captain, June 11, 1861; killed in action at the Battle of Gaines' Mills, Va., June 27, 1862.

JEREMIAH O'NEIL, Captain, assisted in recruiting and organizing the regiment; commissioned Captain, June 11, 1861; killed in action at the Battle of Gaines' Mills, Va., June 27, 1862.

JAMES E. MCCAFFERTY, Captain, assisted in recruiting and organizing the regiment; commissioned First Lieutenant, June 11, 1861; promoted Captain, June 11, 1861; killed in action at the Battle of Gaines' Mills, June 27, 1862.

TIMOTHY O'LEARY, Captain, assisted in recruiting and organizing the regiment; commissioned First Lieutenant, June 11, 1861; promoted Captain, September 7, 1861; mustered out with the regiment; wounded at the Battle of the Wilderness, May 8, 1864; residence, Salem.

Roster of the Officers. 253

John H. Rafferty, Captain, assisted in recruiting and organizing the regiment; commissioned Second Lieutenant, June 11, 1861; promoted First Lieutenant, November 2, 1861; promoted Captain, October 24, 1861; commission cancelled; killed in action at Malvern Hill, July 1, 1862.

John C. Willey, Captain, commissioned Second Lieutenant, June 11, 1861; promoted First Lieutenant, September 11, 1861; promoted Captain, January 28, 1862; discharged, February 7, 1863; residence, Cambridge.

Michael Scanlan, Captain, assisted in recruiting and organizing the regiment; commissioned First Lieutenant, June 11, 1861; promoted Captain, January 28, 1862; wounded at the Battle of Gaines' Mills, June 27, 1862; discharged on account of disability received from wounds, October 19, 1862; residence, Boston.

Thomas K. Roache, Captain, assisted in recruiting and organizing the regiment; commissioned First Lieutenant, June 11, 1861; promoted Captain, July 8, 1862; dismissed, August 3, 1863.

John H. Walsh, Captain, commissioned Second Lieutenant, June 11, 1861; promoted First Lieutenant, June 11, 1861; promoted Captain, January 28, 1862; resigned, January 7, 1863; residence, Boston.

James F. McGonnigle, Captain, assisted in recruiting and organizing the regiment; commissioned First Lieutenant, June 11, 1861; promoted Captain, June 28, 1862; wounded at the Battle of Gaines' Mills, June 27, 1862, and Spottsylvania, Va., May 12, 1862; residence, Stoughton.

Michael F. O'Hara, Captain, assisted in recruiting and organizing the regiment; promoted Second Lieutenant, June 11, 1861; promoted First Lieutenant, February 26, 1862; promoted Captain, June 28, 1862; taken prisoner at the Battle of Gaines' Mills, June 27, 1862; mustered out with the regiment; residence, Boston.

Timothy Burke, Captain, assisted in recruiting and organizing the regiment; commissioned Second Lieutenant, June 11, 1861; promoted First Lieutenant, January 5, 1862; promoted Captain, August 27, 1862; wounded at the Battles of Gaines' Mills, June 27, 1862, and Wilderness, May 5, 1864; mustered out with the regiment; residence, Milford.

Patrick W. Black, Captain, assisted in recruiting and organizing the regiment; enlisted as Commissary Sergeant, June 11, 1861; promoted Second Lieutenant, August 26, 1861; promoted First Lieutenant, March 1, 1862; promoted Captain, October 20, 1862; taken prisoner at the Battle of Gaines' Mills, June 27, 1862; dismissed July 28, 1863; dismissal revoked by the President, and restored to rank, November 10, 1863, but vacancy filled; afterwards appointed Captain, 28th Mass. Vols.; residence, Salem.

WILLIAM A. PHELAN, Captain, enlisted as a private, June 11, 1861; promoted Sergeant; promoted Sergeant Major, November 3, 1861; promoted Second Lieutenant, February 26, 1862; promoted First Lieutenant, July 3, 1862; promoted Captain, June 8, 1863; killed in action at the Battle of the Wilderness, Va.. May 5, 1864.

MICHAEL FLYNN, Captain, assisted in recruiting and organizing the regiment; enlisted as Ordnance Sergeant, June 11, 1861; appointed Drum Major, July, 1861; promoted Sergeant Major, August 26, 1861; promoted Second Lieutenant, October 25, 1861; promoted First Lieutenant, June 28, 1862; promoted Captain, February 8, 1863; mustered out with the regiment; residence, Boston.

MICHAEL A. FINNERTY, Captain, enlisted as a private in Company H, June 11, 1861; promoted Sergeant; promoted Sergeant Major, October 25, 1861; promoted Second Lieutenant, November 3, 1861; promoted First Lieutenant, September 26, 1862; promoted Captain, March 30, 1863; mustered out with the regiment; residence, Milford.

MARTIN O'BRIEN, Captain, enlisted as Sergeant, June 11, 1861; promoted First Sergeant, September 1, 1861; promoted Second Lieutenant, September 26, 1862; promoted First Lieutenant, October 20, 1862; promoted Captain, July 29, 1863; wounded at the Battle of Spottsylvania, Va., May 12, 1864; mustered out with the regiment; residence, Salem.

JAMES W. MACNAMARA, Captain, assisted in recruiting and organizing the regiment; enlisted as Sergeant of Company E, June 11, 1861; appointed Color-bearer, June 11, 1861; promoted First Sergeant, Company I, July 1, 1861; promoted Second Lieutenant, September 26, 1862; promoted First Lieutenant, October 21, 1862; promoted Captain, August 4, 1863; complimented for gallant and meritorious services at the Battles of Hanover Court

House, Va., May 27, 1862, and Gaines' Mills, June 27, 1862, in special orders, by Colonel P. R. Guiney; wounded at the Battle of Gaines' Mills, June 27, 1862, and taken prisoner same day. Mortally wounded at the Battle of the Wilderness, Va., May 5, 1864, and died two hours afterwards; buried at Holyrood Cemetery, Brookline, with military honors.

WILLIAM W. DOHERTY, First Lieutenant, commissioned June 11, 1861; resigned November 1, 1861; residence, Boston.

MICHAEL H. MACNAMARA, First Lieutenant, assisted in recruiting and organizing the regiment; commissioned First Lieutenant, June 11, 1861; discharged November 1, 1861; reënlisted as a private, August 14, 1862; promoted First Sergeant, Company C, September 26, 1862; appointed Acting Provost Marshal, First Division, Fifth Army Corps, November 1, 1862; highly recommended for re-commission by Colonel P. R. Guiney, Ninth Massachusetts Volunteers, General Charles Griffin, commanding First Division, Fifth Army Corps, Colonel McQuade, Fourteenth New York Volunteers, and Colonel Sweitzer, Sixty-Second Pennsylvania Volunteers, but the State authorities refused to make the appointment; the objections, in time, were removed, but the numerical strength of the regiment would not admit of any more promotions; afterwards promoted Quartermaster Sergeant, July 1, 1863; mustered out with the regiment; residence, Boston.

PATRICK WALSH, First Lieutenant, commissioned Second Lieutenant, June 11, 1861; promoted First Lieutenant, August 26, 1861; resigned January 4, 1862; reënlisted as a private, August 14, 1862; promoted First Sergeant, Company E; recommended for re-commission, but the numerical strength of the regiment was not sufficient to admit of any more promotions; mustered out with the regiment; residence, Boston.

PHILIP E. REDMOND, First Lieutenant, assisted in recruiting and organizing the regiment; commissioned Second Lieutenant, June 11, 1861; promoted First Lieutenant, September 7, 1861; cashiered February 28, 1862; reënlisted as a private, August 14, 1862; promoted First Sergeant, Company K, September 10, 1862; promoted Second Lieutenant, March 22, 1863; died of disease, in hospital at Washington, D. C., September 17, 1863.

EDWARD MCSWEENY, First Lieutenant, assisted in recruiting

and organizing the regiment; commissioned Second Lieutenant, June 11, 1861; promoted First Lieutenant, October 25, 1861; killed in action at the Battle of Malvern Hill, Va., July 1, 1862.

RICHARD P. NUGENT, First Lieutenant, assisted in recruiting and organizing the regiment; commissioned Second Lieutenant, June 11, 1861; promoted First Lieutenant, January 28, 1862; killed in action at the Battle of Gaines' Mills, June 27, 1862.

ARCHIBALD SIMPSON, First Lieutenant, assisted in recruiting and organizing the regiment; commissioned Second Lieutenant, June 11, 1861; promoted First Lieutenant, September 26, 1862; killed in action at the Battle of the Wilderness, Va., May 5, 1864.

WILLIAM B. MALONY, First Lieutenant, enlisted as a private, in Company A, June 11, 1861; promoted Commissary Sergeant, November 27, 1861; promoted Second Lieutenant, March 1, 1862; promoted First Lieutenant, September 26, 1862; resigned, March 20, 1863; residence, Boston.

MATTHEW DACEY, First Lieutenant, enlisted as Sergeant in Company B, June 11, 1861; promoted Second Lieutenant, January 5, 1862; promoted First Lieutenant, September 26, 1862; resigned, October 14, 1862; discharged as Second Lieutenant; residence, Boston.

NICHOLAS C. FLAHERTY, First Lieutenant, assisted in recruiting and organizing the regiment; enlisted as First Sergeant in Company D, June 11, 1861; promoted Second Lieutenant, October 24, 1861; promoted First Lieutenant, September 26, 1862; mortally wounded at the Battle of the Wilderness, Va., May 5, 1864; died a few hours afterwards; buried at Holyrood Cemetery, Brookline, with military honors.

JOHN DOHERTY, First Lieutenant, enlisted as a private in Company F, June 11, 1861; promoted Sergeant; promoted Second Lieutenant, February 10, 1862; promoted First Lieutenant, July 2, 1862; discharged, February 12, 1863; wounded at the Battle of Gaines' Mills, Va., June 27, 1862; residence, Salem.

PATRICK E. MURPHY, First Lieutenant, enlisted as First Sergeant, Company H, June 11, 1861; promoted Sergeant Major, in 1862; promoted Second Lieutenant, September 26, 1862; promoted First Lieutenant, February 8, 1863; wounded at the Battle of the Wilderness, May 5, 1864, right arm amputated; mustered out with the regiment; afterwards appointed Lieutenant in the Veteran Reserve Corps; residence, Milford.

BERNARD F. FINAN, First Lieutenant, enlisted as private, Company D, June 11, 1861; promoted, respectively, Corporal, Sergeant, and as First Sergeant, October 24, 1861; promoted Second Lieutenant, September 26, 1862; promoted First Lieutenant, February 13, 1863; wounded at the Battle of the Wilderness, Va., May 5, 1864; mustered out with the regiment; residence, Boston.

ROBERT A. MILLER, First Lieutenant, assisted in recruiting and organizing the regiment; enlisted as First Sergeant, Company B, June 11, 1861; promoted Second Lieutenant, August 27, 1862; promoted First Lieutenant, March 21, 1863; dismissed as Second Lieutenant, August 3, 1863; residence, Boston.

TIMOTHY DACEY, First Lieutenant, enlisted as private, Company I, June 11, 1861; promoted respectively Corporal and Sergeant, in 1861; promoted Second Lieutenant, September 26, 1862; promoted First Lieutenant, April 7, 1863; wounded at the Battle of the Wilderness, May 5, 1864, but remained in command of his company; mustered out with the regiment; residence, Lawrence.

JOHN F. DOHERTY, First Lieutenant, assisted in recruiting and organizing the regiment; enlisted as Sergeant, Company A, June 11, 1861; promoted Commissary Sergeant, February 10, 1862; promoted Quartermaster Sergeant, March 10, 1862; promoted Sergeant Major, June 20, 1862; promoted Second Lieutenant, September 26, 1862; promoted First Lieutenant, March 30, 1863; wounded at the Battles of Malvern Hill, Va., July 1, 1862, and Wilderness, May 5, 1864; mustered out with the regiment; residence, Boston.

JOSEPH MURPHY, First Lieutenant, enlisted as Sergeant, Company F, June 11, 1861; promoted Quartermaster Sergeant in 1862; promoted Second Lieutenant, April 1, 1863; promoted First Lieutenant, August 4, 1863; wounded at the Battle of the Wilderness, May 5, 1864, but remained in command of his company; mustered out with the regiment; residence, Salem.

JAMES O'DONNELL, First Lieutenant, enlisted as a recruit, 1862; promoted Second Lieutenant, February 8, 1863; promoted First Lieutenant, July 29, 1863; mustered out with the regiment; residence, Salem.

WILLIAM R. BURKE, First Lieutenant, enlisted as Sergeant,

Company H, June 11, 1861; promoted Second Lieutenant, January 8, 1863; promoted First Lieutenant, August 4, 1863; mustered out with the regiment; residence, Milford.

TIMOTHY F. LEE, Second Lieutenant, assisted in recruiting and organizing the regiment; commissioned Second Lieutenant, June 11, 1861; dismissed, November 2, 1861; residence, Boston.

EDWARD FINNOTTIE, Second Lieutenant, assisted in recruiting and organizing the regiment; enlisted as First Sergeant, Company G, June 11, 1861; promoted Second Lieutenant, September, 11, 1861; discharged, March 31, 1862; residence, Boston.

FRANCIS O'DOWD, Second Lieutenant, assisted in recruiting and organizing the regiment; enlisted as Sergeant, June 11, 1861; appointed Color Bearer, June 11, 1861; promoted Second Lieutenant, February 10, 1862; killed in action, at the Battle of Gaines' Mills, Va., June 27, 1862.

CHARLES B. MCGINNISKIN, Second Lieutenant, enlisted as private, Company D, promoted respectively Corporal and Sergeant; and as Second Lieutenant, September 26, 1862; wounded at the Battle of the Wilderness, Va., May 5, 1864; leg amputated, died a few days after at Fredericksburg Hospital.

WILLIAM J. BLOOD, Second Lieutenant, enlisted as a recruit, August 11, 1862; promoted Second Lieutenant, September 26, 1862; discharged for physical disability, August 10, 1863; residence, Boston.

HUGH MCGONNIGLE, Second Lieutenant, enlisted as First Sergeant, Company K, June 11, 1861; promoted Second Lieutenant, October 21, 1862; discharged, February 28, 1863; residence, Stoughton.

FRANK M. LALOR, Second Lieutenant, enlisted as a recruit, in 1862; promoted Second Lieutenant, February 13, 1863; dismissed, August 3, 1863; residence, Lawrence.

WILLIAM A. PLUNKETT, Second Lieutenant, enlisted as a recruit, August 14, 1862; promoted Second Lieutenant, March 1, 1863; wounded at the Battle of the Wilderness, May 5, 1864; mustered out with the regiment; residence, Boston.

JAMES O'NEIL, Second Lieutenant, enlisted as Sergeant, Company B, June 11, 1861; promoted First Sergeant, August 27, 1862; promoted Second Lieutenant, April 8, 1863; killed at the Battle of Laurel Hill, Va., May 9, 1864; residence, Boston.

RECAPITULATION.

No. of officers mustered out on expiration of term of service, . 24
" " " killed in battle, ... 13
" " " " by accident, ... 1
" " " died of wounds received in battle, ... 2
" " " " of disease, ... *2
" " " discharged to accept promotion in other corps, . 3
" " " discharged for disability, ... 3
" " " discharged, ... 4
" " " dismissed, ... 6
" " " cashiered, ... †1
" " " resigned, ... 15

Whole No. of officers, ... 74

* One officer cashiered, who reënlisted, was promoted and died of disease.
† Afterwards re-enlisted and recommended for commission.

ROSTER OF ENLISTED MEN

OF THE

NINTH REGIMENT MASS. VOL. INFANTRY.

NON-COMMISSIONED STAFF.

William Strachan, Sergeant Major, discharged to accept commission. (See Officers' Roster.)

Michael Flynn, Sergeant Major, discharged to accept commission. (See Officers' Roster.)

Michael A. Finnerty, Sergeant Major, discharged to accept commission. (See Officers' Roster.)

William A. Phelan, Sergeant Major, discharged to accept commission. (See Officers' Roster.)

P. E. Murphy, Sergeant Major, discharged to accept commission. (See Officers' Roster.)

William R. Burke, Sergeant Major, discharged to accept commission. (See Officers' Roster.)

Nathan Carns, Sergeant Major, mustered out June 21, 1864.

Thomas Mooney, Quartermaster Sergeant, discharged to accept commission. (See Officers' Roster.)

John F. Doherty, Quartermaster Sergeant, discharged to accept commission. (See Officers' Roster.)

Joseph Murphy, Quartermaster Sergeant, discharged to accept commission. (See Officers' Roster.)

M. H. Macnamara, Quartermaster Sergeant; reënlisted; mustered out June 21, 1864. (See Officers' Roster.)

P. W. Black, Commissary Sergeant, discharged to accept commission. (See Officers' Roster.)

William B. Maloney, Commissary Sergeant, discharged to accept commission. (See Officers' Roster.)

Frank O'Dowd, Commissary Sergeant, discharged to accept commission. (See Officers' Roster.)

Daniel G. Macnamara, Commissary Sergeant, discharged to accept commission. (See Officers' Roster.)

Joseph H. Monaghan, Commissary Sergeant, reënlisted, and transferred to Thirty-second Massachusetts Volunteers.

Reed B. Granger, Hospital Steward, discharged by order of General McClellan; afterwards appointed Acting Volunteer Surgeon.

Joseph A. Sullivan, Hospital Steward, mustered out June 21, 1864.

REGIMENTAL BAND.*

Michael O'Connor, Leader, discharged, per order of the War Department, at Harrison's Landing, Va., dated June 30, 1862.

William H. Graham, Musician, discharged, per order of the War Department, at Harrison's Landing, Va., dated June 30, 1862.

Lewis Boles, Musician, discharged, per order of the War Department, at Harrison's Landing, Va., dated June 30, 1862.

John Litch, Musician, discharged, per order of the War Department, at Harrison's Landing, Va., dated June 30, 1862; wounded at the Battle of Malvern Hill, Va., July 1, 1862.

Earnest Wood, Musician, discharged, per order of the War Department, at Harrison's Landing, Va., dated June 30, 1862.

Victor Gibson, Musician, discharged, per order of the War Department, at Harrison's Landing, Va., dated June 30, 1862.

William Tinery, Musician, discharged, per order of the War Department, at Harrison's Landing, Va., dated June 30, 1862.

Martin McCabe, Musician, discharged, per order of the War Department, at Harrison's Landing, Va., dated June 30, 1862.

Edwin Duryea, Musician, discharged, per order of the War Department, at Harrison's Landing, Va., dated June 30, 1862.

John Murray, Musician, discharged, per order of the War Department, at Harrison's Landing, Va., dated June 30, 1862.

---

* Mustered out of service, August 10, 1862, at Harrison's Landing, Va.

Patrick Fitzgerald, Musician, discharged, per order of the War Department, at Harrison's Landing, Va., dated June 30, 1862.

George A. Gastin, Musician, discharged, per order of the War Department, at Harrison's Landing, Va., dated June 30, 1862.

William A. Knight, Musician, discharged, per order of the War Department, at Harrison's Landing, Va., dated June 30, 1862.

John Higgins, Musician, discharged, per order of the War Department, at Harrison's Landing, Va., dated June 30, 1862.

Thomas E. Ward, Musician, discharged, per order of the War Department, at Harrison's Landing, Va., dated June 30, 1862.

Charles L. Flint, Musician, discharged, per order of the War Department, at Harrison's Landing, Va., dated June 30, 1862.

A. K. P. Rounds, Musician, discharged for disability, September 16, 1861.

James Scanlan, Musician, discharged, per Special Order No. 91, December 16, 1861.

Thomas Russell, Musician, discharged, per Special Order No. 91, December 16, 1861.

John Mulvene, Musician, discharged, per Special Order No. 91, December 16, 1861.

Thomas Mulvene, Musician, discharged, per Special Order No. 91, December 16, 1861.

Peter Dunn, Musician, discharged, per Special Order No. 91, December 16, 1861.

Frank Damon, Musician, discharged for disability, January 15, 1862.

Company A.

Bartholomew Kallaher, First Sergeant, mustered out June 21, 1864.
Charles R. Warren,	Sergeant,	"	"	"
Daniel Mullane,	"	"	"	"
Donald Ross,	"	"	"	"
John McLaughlin,	Corporal,	"	"	"
Daniel Kenney,	"	"	"	"
Michael McLaughlin,	"	"	"	"
John O'Donnell,	"	"	"	"
Patrick Gallagher,	"	"	"	"
William Tracy,	Wagoner,	"	"	"
Bellows, John,	Private,	"	"	"

COMPANY A — *continued.*

Brady, Edward,	Private,	mustered out June 21, 1864.
Bayley, Ralph,	"	" " " "
Carmody, Cornelius,	"	" " " "
Cummings, James,	"	" " " "
Cass, Thomas,	"	" " " "
Cronan, Maurice,	"	" " " "
Cunis, John,	"	" " " "
Ford, Thomas,	"	" " " "
Flynn, Edward,	"	" " " "
Gardiner, William C.	"	" " " "
Hagan, Patrick,	"	" " " "
Hagarty, Patrick,	"	" " " "
Hickey, James,	"	" " " "
Lynch, John,	"	" " " "
Lawler John,	"	" " " "
McLaughlin, Terrence,	"	" " " "
Moore, Alexander,	"	" " " "
McMahon, Thomas,	"	" " " "
McGennisken, Thomas, Jr.,	"	" " " "
Ninan, Daniel,	"	" " " "
O'Hara, John B.,	"	" " " "
O'Hara, John P.,	"	" " " "
Riley, Simon J.,	"	" " " "
Sheehan, Timothy,	"	" " " "
White, William,	"	" " " "
Wyman, Henry,	"	" " " "
Ward, Thomas F.,	"	" " " "
Walsh, Patrick,	"	" " " "

DISCHARGED.

Burke, Patrick,	Corporal,	for disability,	February	2, 1862.
Boynton, Vassal P.,	Private,	"	March	23, 1863.
Coughlin, Jeremiah,	"	"	September	24, 1862.
Carroll, Thomas,	"	"	August	18, 1861.
Cryan, Patrick,	"	"	January	30, 1862.
Dwyre, John,	"	"	November	24, "
Donovan, Patrick,	"	"		
Deboa, James,	"	"	October	29, "
Donovan, John,	"	"	September	29, "

Company A — *continued.*

Edwards, George,	Private,	for disability,	January	16, 1862.
Fitzgerald, James,	"	"	December	29, "
Flaherty, William,	"	"		
Henley Edward,	"	"	October	19, "
Hennessy, John,	"	"	August	18, 1861.
Hanary, John,	"	"	November	14, 1862.
Lovett, Charles,	"	"	September	27, "
Lewellen, Thomas,	"	"	February	21, 1863.
McDermott, Michael,	Sergeant,	"	September	6, 1862.
Mulligan, Thomas,	Private,	"	December	18, "
McGlone, Charles,	"	"	February	24, 1863.
Moore James,	"	"		
McCarthy, John,	"	"	June	16, "
Murphy, Peter,	"	"	March	1, 1864.
Meehan, Michael,	"	"	October	29, 1862.
McGowen, Edward,	"	"	"	"
McNamara, Owen,	"	"	"	"
Noonan, Edward,	"	"	March	10, 1864.
O'Reilley, James,	"	"	April	17, 1863.
O'Brien, Peter,	"	"	August	30, 1862.
O'Callaghan, William F.,	"	"	March	5, 1863.
Odey, William B.,	"	"	October	6, 1863.
Powers, Benjamin,	"	"	"	22, 1862.
Phillips, Robert,	"	"	August	25, 1863.
Quinn, William,	"	"	September	26, 1862.
Sheridan, Bernard,	"	"	November	5, "
Sullivan, Daniel,	"	"	February	15, 1864.
Semple, Robert,	"	"	December	24, 1862.
Sparrow, Philip O.,	"	"	"	16, 1863.
Taylor, Bartholomew,	"	"	November	22, 1862.
Thornton, John,	"	"	"	2, "
Young, Austin,	"	"	December	15, 1863.
Walsh, James,	"	"	"	"

Transferred.

John F. Doherty,	1st Sergeant,	to Non.-Com. Staff,	Feb.	10, 1862.
William B. Maloney,	"	" "	Aug.	26, 1861.
William A. Phalen,	"	" "	Nov.	3, "

Company A — continued.

Adams, William,	Private,	to Company H.
Burke, James,	"	to Vet. Res. Corps.
Brown, Jonathan,	"	to 32d Mass. Vols., June 9, 1864.
Bradley, William,	"	" " " "
Burke, John H.,	"	" " " "
Feyle, Bernard,	"	" " " "
Griffin, Michael,	"	" " " "
Kelley John,	"	to Bat. D, 5th U.S. Art., Oct. 25, 1862.
Lally, Daniel,	"	to 32d Mass. Vols., June 9, 1864.
Murphy, John,	"	to Company E.
Moakler, John,	"	to 32d Mass. Vols., June 9, 1864.
McCarville, Patrick,	"	" " " "
Ninan, Jeremiah,	"	" " " "
O'Leary, Daniel,	"	" " " "
O'Brien, John,	"	" " " "
Palmer, William E.,	"	to Company E.
Parker Edwin S.,	"	to 32d Mass. Vols., June 9, 1864.
Reynolds, John A.,	"	" " " "
Rodman, William C.,	"	" " " "
Sullivan, Patrick,	"	to Company I.
Sweeney, Charles,	"	to 32d Mass. Vols., June 9, 1864.
Stimson, John A.,	"	" " " "
Smith, Henry,	"	" " " "
Smith, Peter,	"	" " " "
Tirrell, George J.,	"	" " " "
Ulhaas, John,	"	" " " "
Webber, John,	"	" " " "
Wilson, George,	"	" " " "
Zeigler, David,	"	to Battery D, 5th U. S. Artillery.

DECEASED.

Aaron, Otis F., Private, died March 15, 1862.
Buckley, David, Private, drowned June 23, 1861.
Brown, John, Private, died December 6, 1862.
Davis, William, Private, died.
Doherty, James, Private, killed at the Battle of Gaines' Mills, Va., June 27, 1862.
Early, Patrick, Sergeant, killed at the Battle of Malvern Hill, Va., July 1, 1862.

Company A — *continued.*

Foley, James, Private, killed at the Battle of Gaines's Mills, Va., June 27, 1862.

Gleason, John, Private, killed at the Battle of Gaines' Mills, Va., June 27, 1862.

Garrity, Michael, Private, died January 28, 1863.

Glynn, Thomas, Private, killed at the Battle of Spottsylvania Court House, May 12, 1864.

Heutch, Christopher, Private, died November 26, 1862.

Kennedy, Daniel, Private, died from wounds, July 14, 1862.

Keating, Patrick, Private, killed at the Battle of Gaines' Mills, Va., June 27, 1862.

Keenan, Edward, Private, killed at the Battle of Spottsylvania Court House, Va., May 12, 1864.

Lynch, Maurice, Corporal, killed at the Battle of Gaines' Mills, Va., June 27, 1862.

McIntire, Peter, Private, killed at the Battle of Gaines' Mills, Va., June 27, 1862.

McGuire, James, Private, killed at the Battle of Gaines' Mills, Va., June 27, 1862.

McGlone, Hugh, Private, killed at the Battle of Malvern Hill, Va., July 1, 1862.

Manning, John, Private, killed at the Battle of Gaines' Mills, Va., June 27, 1862.

Melanfry, Paul, Private, killed at the Battle of Gaines' Mills, Va., June 27, 1862.

McDonald, Angers, Private, died March 25, 1864.

Nicholson, John, Private, killed at the Battle of Malvern Hill, Va., July 1, 1862.

O'Reilly, Thomas, Private, killed at the Battle of Malvern Hill, Va., July 1, 1862.

O'Keefe, David, Private, died June 23, 1863.

Pope, Roger, Private, killed at the Battle of Gaines' Mills, Va., June 27, 1862.

Lanigan, Peter, Private, killed at the Battle of Spottsylvania Court House, Va., May 12, 1864.

Slevin, Hugh, Private, killed at the Battle of Spottsylvania Court House, May 12, 1864.

Teirnon, Hugh, Private, killed at the Battle of Gaines' Mills, Va., June 27, 1862.

Company A — *continued.*

Fitzgerald, Thomas, Sergeant, killed at the Battle of Wilderness, May 5, 1864.

Missing.

Comerford, John,	Private,	in action,	November 28, 1863.	
Coffey, John,	"	"	May	5, 1864.
McClosky, Paul,	Corporal,	"	"	12, "
Shahan, Edward,	"	"	"	12, "

(Deserters dropped from the rolls.)

Company B.

Henry B. O'Neil,	First Sergeant, mustered out June 21, 1864.			
Patrick H. Brickley,	Sergeant,	"	"	"
John W. Cullenan,	"	"	"	"
Bernard Lane,	"	"	"	"
James Remick,	"	"	"	"
William Dooley,	Corporal,	"	"	"
David Goulding,	"	"	"	"
John Burns,	"	"	"	"
James Battesby,	"	"	"	"
Michael Fallon,	"	"	"	"
Daniel Fallon	Wagoner,	"	"	"
Boyle, Patrick,	Private,	"	"	"
Cumming, Martin,	"	"	"	"
Connell, Peter,	"	"	"	"
Curren, John,	"	"	"	"
Cullenan, John,	"	"	"	"
Driscoll, Dennis,	"	"	"	"
Danahay, Patrick,	"	"	"	"
Farley, John,	"	"	"	"
McGurrien, Michael,	"	"	"	"
Murphy, Martin,	"	"	"	"
McCarthy, John,	"	"	"	"
McCarthy, Dennis,	"	"	"	"
McKeirnan, John,	"	"	"	"
McNulty, James,	"	"	"	"
O'Brien, Michael,	"	"	"	"

COMPANY B — *continued.*

Rice, Sylvester,	Private, mustered out June 21, 1864.	
Schofield, Peter,	" " " "	
Sullivan, Timothy,	" " " "	
Sullivan, Michael,	" " " "	
Toomey, Maurice,	" " " "	
Tracey, William,	" " " "	
Whelan, Michael,	" " " "	

DISCHARGED.

Matthew Dacey, Sergeant, to accept commission, January 5, 1862. (See Officers' Roster.)

Robert A. Miller, First Sergeant, to accept commission, August 27, 1862. (See Officers' Roster.)

James O'Neill, Sergeant, to accept commission, April 8, 1863. (See Officers' Roster.)

Michael Brannon,	Corporal, for disability,	August	20, 1864.
Adams, George,	Private, "	August	8, 1863.
Callahan, John,	" "	Oct. 10, 1862; from wounds.	
Brett, John,	Private, for disability,	August	18, 1861.
Burke, John B.,	" "	"	30, 1862.
Bresnehan, John,	" "	January,	10, 1863.
Burns, John, 3d,	" "	"	12, "
Buckley, James,	" "	"	29, "
Barker, Thomas,	Sergeant, "	August	10, 1862.
Baney, John,	" "	January	28, 1864.
Driscoll, Timothy,	Private, "	September	30, 1862.
Daily, Daniel J.,	" "	October	30, "
Donovan, John, 2d,	" "	"	" "
Dugan, William,	" "	September	28, 1863.
Emerson, Amos,	" "	December	16, "
Farley, Patrick,	" "	June	15, "
Griffin, Michael,	" "	February	2, "
Gleason, Michael,	" "	November	20, 1862.
Greary, George,	" "	April	16, 1863.
Hall, William,	" "	October	14, 1862.

Hernan, John, Private, for disability, November 20, 1862; from wounds.

Horan, Dennis, Private, for disability, July 31, 1863.

COMPANY B. —continued.

Lyons, Charles, Private, for disability, October 16, 1862; from wounds.
Lamb, Owen J.,   Private, for disability, December 25, 1863.
Leach, Elbridge,   "   "   March 26, 1864.
McDonald, Donald,   "   "   January 6, 1863.
Martin, John, Private, for disability, January 12, 1863; from wounds.
McLaughlin, Patrick, Private, for disability, January 19, 1863.
McGovern, Phillip, Private, for disability, January 19, 1863; from wounds.
McGuire, John,   Private, for disability, December 21, 1863.
Naughton, Thomas,   "   "   October, 30, "
Newton, Thomas, Private, for disability, February 24, 1863; from wounds.
Palmer, John N., Private, for disability, January, 20, 1863.
Powers, Thomas, Private, for disability, February 9, 1863; from wounds.
Pearce, Charles E., Private, for disability, December 11, 1863.
Quinlan, Thomas, Private, for disability, February 4, 1863; from wounds.
Sheridan, Patrick, Private, for disability, March 10, 1862; from wounds.
Somerville, Alexander, Private, for disability, October 23, 1861.
Sullivan, William, Private, for disability, September 20, 1862; from wounds.
Smith, William, Private, for disability, December, 3, 1862; from wounds.
Scanlan, Joseph F.,   Private, for disability, February 23, 1863.
Turish, Hugh,   "   "   August 18, 1861.
Thompson, William,   "   "   September 26, "
Welch, James N.,   "   "   October 30, 1862.

TRANSFERRED.

Adams, Carl,   Private, to 32d Mass. Volunteers, June 9, 1864.
Brennan, Joseph,   "   "   "   "
Brown, Joseph,   "   "   "   "
Butler, Hercules,   "   "   "   "
Bushe, Otto,   "   "   "   "

COMPANY B — *continued.*

Busse, William, Private, to 32d Mass. Vols., June 9, 1864.
Bacon, William F., " " " "
Burke, James, " " " "
Geblin, James, " " " "
Grant, James, " " " "
Gleason, Michael, " " " "
Hart, Patrick, " " " "
Howard, Martin, " " " "
Joyce, Taylor, " " " "
Kenny, Thomas, " " " "
Longrein, Charles, " " " "
Maybie, Francis, " " " "
Macul, Stephen J., " " " "
McCoy, James, " " " "
Powers, Edward, " " " "
Stelfok, James F., " " " "
Walsh, John, " " " "
Barker, Owen, " to Vet. Res. Corps, November 27, 1863.
Griffin, John, " " " September 12, "
Phelan Thomas " " " " 26, "

DECEASED.

Archpool, Lawrence, Private, killed at Battle of Laurel Hill, Va., May 8, 1864.

Burns, James, Private, died of disease, September 27, 1862.

Bresnehan, John, Private, killed at the Battle of Laurel Hill, Va., May 8, 1864.

Conlan, Andrew, Private, killed at the Battle of Gaines' Mills, Va., June 27, 1862.

Cullennan, John, Private, killed at the Battle of Gaines' Mills, Va., June 27, 1862.

Creighton, Michael C., Sergeant, killed at the Battle of Laurel Hill, Va., May 8, 1864.

Crossin, Eugene, Private, died at Andersonville Prison, Aug. 10, 1864.

Carney, William, Private, killed at the Battle of Laurel Hill, Va., May 8, 1864.

Doherty, Daniel, Private, killed at the Battle of Gaines' Mills, Va., June 27, 1862.

Company B — *continued.*

Ferris, John, Private, killed at the Battle of Laurel Hill, Va., May 8, 1864.
Gordon, Joseph, Private, killed at the Battle of Mechanicsville, Va., June 26, 1862.
Hyde, Dennis, Private, killed at the Battle of Gaines' Mills, Va., June 27, 1862.
Hogan, Thomas, Private, killed at the Battle of Gaines' Mills, Va., June 27, 1862.
Keenan, Michael, Private, killed at the Battle of Gaines' Mills, Va., June 27, 1862.
Kelly, Patrick, Private, killed at the Battle Laurel Hill, Va., May 8, 1864.
McQuade, John, Private, killed at the Battle of Gaines' Mills, Va., June 27, 1862.
Meany, Thomas, Sergeant, killed at the Battle of Malvern Hill, Va., July 1, 1862.
McGavigan, Patrick, Private, killed at the Battle of Gaines' Mills, Va., June 27, 1862.
O'Brien, John, Private, killed at the Battle of Gaines' Mills, Va., June 27, 1862.
Regan, John, Private, killed at the Battle of the Wilderness, Va., May 5, 1864.
Smith, Matthew, Private, killed at the Battle of Malvern Hill, Va., July 1, 1862.
Sheehan, Martin, Private, killed at the Battle of the Wilderness, Va., May 5, 1862.
Thompson, Charles, Private, killed at the Battle of Malvern Hill, Va., July 1, 1862.
Ward, James, Private, killed at the Battle of the Wilderness, Va., May 5, 1864.

Company C.

John P. Murphy,	First Sergeant, mustered out June 21, 1864.	
James Petty,	" " " "	
William Reynolds,	" " " "	
James D. Gallagher,	" " " "	
Edward McLaughlin,	" " " "	
Thomas Barnes,	Corporal, " " "	

COMPANY C — *continued.*

Maurice O'Donnell,	Corporal,	mustered out June 21, 1864.		
James Murray,	"	"	"	"
Boylston, Michael,	Private,	"	"	"
Campbell, John,	"	"	"	"
Coyne, John,	"	"	"	"
Creig, William,	"	"	"	"
Coleman, Thomas,	"	"	"	"
Connolly, Michael,	"	"	"	"
Corcoran, Daniel,	"	"	"	"
Flynn, William,	"	"	"	"
Ford, Michael,	"	"	"	"
Gilles, James,	"	"	"	"
Hennebry, John,	"	"	"	"
Harty, Michael,	"	"	"	"
Howard, Thomas,	"	"	"	"
Jones, Patrick,	"	"	"	"
Lynch, John,	"	"	"	"
Mullen, William,	"	"	"	"
McTighe, Anthony,	"	"	"	"
McQueeny, William,	"	"	"	"
McGovern, James,	"	"	"	"
O'Toole, Michael,	"	"	"	"
O'Brien, William,	"	"	"	"
O'Brien, Timothy,	"	"	"	"
Regan, John,	"	"	"	"
Ring, John,	"	"	"	"
Ryan, John, 1st,	"	"	"	"
Ryan, John, 2d,	"	"	"	"
Slattery, James,	"	"	"	"
Shannahan, Robert,	"	"	"	"
Sullivan, Michael,	"	"	"	"
Sheehan, Cornelius,	"	"	"	"

DISCHARGED.

Christopher Plunkett, Sergeant, to accept commission, September 26, 1862. (See Officers' Roster.)

William A. Plunkett, Sergeant, to accept commission, March 1, 1863. (See Officers' Roster.)

Company C — *continued*.

Frank M. Lalor, Sergeant, to accept commission, February 13, 1863. (See Officers' Roster.)

Brett, Michael, Private, for disability, October 13, 1862.

Cosgrove, John, Private, for disability, October 28, 1861, from wounds.

Cullen, Michael,	Private, for disability,	October	1, 1862.
Conniff, John,	" "	"	29, "
Clancy, William,	" "	May	7, 1863.
Conant, Daniel M.,	" "	December	11, 1863.
Cushing, Andrew J.,	" "	"	"
Casey, James,	" "	October	29, 1862.
Delaney, Michael,	" "	December	11, 1863.
Dudley, Henry E.,	" War Dept. order,	"	12, "
Fegan, Lawrence,	" for disability,	November	3, 1862.
Ford, Edward,	" "	March	30, 1863.
Fahey, William,	" "	"	29, "
Farrington, Hugh,	" "	August	18, 1861.
Gilldey, Patrick,	" "	February	2, 1863.
Goslin, James,	" "	November	3, 1862.
Harvey, John,	" "	February	9, 1863.
Harrington, Andrew,	" "	August	18, 1861.
Hatch, George E.,	" "	December	11, 1863.
Kerr, William,	" "	March	18, 1862.

from wounds.

Kendall, John H.,	" "	December	11, 1863.
Lord, Charles W.,	" "	August	10, 1861.
Lyons, Michael,	" "	"	22, 1862.

from accidental wounds.

Matthews, John F.,	Private, "	March	8, "
Murphy, Thomas,	" "	October	30, "
Murphy, James,	" "	"	22, "
Murphy, Jeremiah,	" "	March	11, 1863,

from wounds.

Murray, Charles,	" "	. "	" "
Murphy, Michael B.,	" "	October	22, 1862.
McDonald, Charles H.,	" "	March	8, "
McCaffery, John,	" "	October	3, "
McAuliff, Thomas,	" "	December,	"

Company C — *continued.*

McGin, Patrick,	Private, for disability,	March,	1863.
Montague, Daniel,	" "	"	"
McGuire, John D.,	" "	"	6, 1862, from wounds.
McMahon, Thomas,	" "	December 9,	" from wounds.
McNamara, Michael S.,	" "	January	16, 1863, from wounds.
Mahoney, Frank,	" "	December 11,	"
O'Brien, William,	" "	October	11, 1862.
O'Brien, John,	" "	March	18, "
Perodi, Domingo,	" "	"	10, "
Powers, John, 1st,	" "	"	10, "
Powers, Patrick,	" "	"	10, "
Pym, William,	" "	"	21, "
Pierce, John,	" "	December 11, 1863.	
Patterson, George,	" on writ *hab. corp.*,	"	13, 1862.
Ryan, John,	" for disability,	October	18, 1861.
Ryan, Patrick,	" "	"	15; "
Sendow, Henry,	" "	March	6, 1863.
Williams, George,	" "	October	22, 1862.
Bannon, Thomas,	" "		
Leonard, John,	" "	January	25, 1863.

Transferred.

Burke, William,	Private, to 32d Mass. Vols., June 9, 1864
Burke, Martin,	" Vet. Res. Corps, Sept. 30, 1863.
Cooney, Jeremiah,	" Company —, Oct. 3, "
Casey, Michael,	" " I, " 3, "
Coy, George H.,	" 32d Mass. Vols., June 9, 1864.
Coffee, Michael,	" " " "
Campbell, William,	" " " "
Clancy, John,	" " " "
Coyle, James,	" Vet. Res. Corps, Oct. 1, 1863.
Dyer, Daniel,	" 32d Mass. Vols., June 9, 1864.
Elliott, George H.,	" Vet. Res. Corps, Feb. 27, "
Sheehan, Daniel J.,	" 32d Mass. Vols., June 9, "
Foye, William,	" " " "

ROSTER OF ENLISTED MEN.

COMPANY C — continued.

Flanagan, Henry,	Private, to 32d Mass. Vols.,	June	9, 1864.
Frost, Benjamin,	"	"	"	"
Fields, Simon,	"	"	"	"
Gleason, Spencer W.,	"	"	"	"
Gaffney, George,	"	"	"	"
Jones, William,	"	Vet. Res. Corps, Sept. 30, 1863.
Kelley, James,	"	32d Mass. Vols., June 9, 1864.
Kelleher, John,	"	"	"	"
McNamara, Michael H.,	1st Sergt., to N. C. S. (See Officers' Roster.)
McCarthy, James,	Sergt., to 32d Mass. Vols., June 9, 1864.
Martin, Daniel,	Corporal,	"	"	"
Maloney, Thomas,	Private,	"	"	"
O'Mahoney, Daniel,	"	"	"	"
Phinney, Edwin,	Corporal,	"	"	"
Parker, John H.,	Private,	"	"	"
Parker, Warren,	"	"	"	"
Sullivan, Dennis,	"	"	"	"
Somerville, Alexander,	"	to Vet. Res. Corps, Dec. 16, 1863.
Wright, George,	"	to 32d Mass. Vols., June 9, 1864.
Walsh, Edward,	"	"	"	"
Walsh, Daniel,	Corporal,	"	"	"

DECEASED.

Dolan, Michael, Private, killed at the battle of the Wilderness, Va., May 5, 1864.

Dennison, John, Private, died, November 7, 1863.

Duncan, Charles, Private, killed at battle of Malvern Hill, Va., July 1, 1862.

Flanagan, John, Private, killed at the battle of the Wilderness, Va., May 5, 1864.

Greeney, Charles, Private, killed at the battle of Gaines' Mills, Va., June 27, 1862.

Grier, George, Sergeant, killed at the battle of Gaines' Mills, Va., June 27, 1862.

Hughes, James, Corporal, killed at the battle of Gaines' Mills, Va., June 27, 1862.

Harrell, John, Private, killed at the battle of Spottsylvania Court House, Va., May 19, 1864.

COMPANY C — *continued.*

Hyde, John, Private, killed at the battle of Gaines' Mills, Va., June 27, 1862.
Leary, Daniel, Corporal, killed at the battle of Gaines' Mills, Va., June 27, 1862.
Madden, Erasmus D, Private, killed at the battle of the Wilderness, Va., May 5, 1864.
McGee, Patrick, Sergeant, killed at the battle of Gaines' Mills, Va., June 27, 1862.
Petty, Edward, Private, killed at the battle of the Wilderness, Va., May 5, 1864.
Sheehan, James, Private, killed at the battle of Malvern Hill, Va., July 1, 1862.
Slattery, Michael, Private, killed at the battle of Gaines' Mills, Va., June 27, 1864.
Waters, John, Private, died of wounds, November 5, 1862.
Walder, Henry, Private, killed at the battle of Spottsylvania Court House, Va., May 12, 1864.

(Deserters dropped.)

Company D.

James Cavanagh,	Sergeant,	mustered out June 21, 1864.		
James Murray,	"	"	"	"
Thomas Collins,	"	"	"	"
Peter Doran,	Corporal,	"	"	"
Peter Rodgers,	"	"	"	"
William Hangley,	"	"	"	"
Thomas Mollahan,	"	"	"	"
James Hughes,	Wagoner,	"	"	"
Simon P. Hickey,	Musician,	"	"	"
Baldwin, George,	Private,	"	"	"
Blanchard, Henry,	"	"	"	"
Burke, Cuthbert,	"	"	"	"
Carr, James, 1st,	"	"	"	"
Childs, Albert,	"	"	"	"
Clancy, Jeremiah,	"	"	"	"
Conlon, Thomas,	"	"	"	"

COMPANY D — *continued.*

Coakley, Dennis,	Private,	mustered out, June 21, 1864.
Coughlin, Joseph,	"	" " " "
Devlin, John,	"	" " " "
Doherty, Edward,	"	" " " "
Doherty, Anthony,	"	" " " "
Farrell, James,	"	" " " "
Flemming, James,	"	" " " "
Giles, George,	"	" " " ".
Jameson, John A.,	"	" " " "
Lynch, George,	"	" " " "
Marshall, James T.,	"	" " " "
Masterson, John,	"	" " " "
Meadon, Albert,	"	" " " "
Mellen, William,	"	" " " "
McDermott, William,	"	" " " "
Murphy, Jeremiah,	"	" " " "
Murray, Daniel A.,	"	" " " "
Plant, Joseph,	"	" " " "
Quigley, James,	"	" " " "
Roach, Michael,	"	" " " "
Shea, Jeremiah,	"	" " " "
Shields, William,	"	" " " "
Sweeny, William,	"	" " " "
Young, Nicholas,	"	" " " "

DISCHARGED.

Nicholas C. Flaherty, 1st Sergeant, to accept commission, October 24, 1861. (See Officers' Roster.)

Bernard F. Finan, 1st Sergeant, to accept commission, September 26, 1862. (See Officers' Roster.)

Charles B. McGinniskin, 1st Sergeant, to accept commission, September 26, 1862. (See Officers' Roster.)

James O'Donnell, Sergeant, to accept commission, February 8, 1863. (See Officers' Roster.)

Edward McDonald, Sergeant, ——, March 23, 1863.

Benway, Augustus, Private, from hospital, ——

Brown, Dennis, Private, for disability, October 17, 1862; from wounds.

Company D — *continued.*

Burt, Samuel,	Private,	for disability,	December 11, 1863.
Clancy, Michael,	"	"	November 19, 1862; from wounds.
Collins, John,	"	"	———
Crowley, Jeremiah,	"	"	October 3, 1862.
Condon, Michael,	"	"	———
Conlon, Michael,	"	"	February 2, 1862.
Cummings, James,	"	"	———
Daley, Frank,	"	"	September 20, 1861.
Donohoe, John,	"	"	October 23, 1861.
Duffy, Bernard,	"	"	December 28, 1863; from wounds.
Dugan, Dennis,	"	"	October 29, 1862.
Good, John P.,	"	"	April 25, 1863; from wounds.
Gleason, John,	"	"	October 23, 1861.
Haverlin, Hugh,	"	"	February 15, 1863.
Healey, Dennis,	"	"	October 29, 1863.
Heenan, John C.,	"	"	December 10, 1862.
Hinckley, John,	"	"	March 10, 1863.
Keefe, John,	"	by order of War Department,	———
Kelleher, John,	"	for disability,	November 28, 1862.
Lynch, William,	"	"	December 19, 1862.
Mahoney, John,	"	"	October 28, 1862.
Maloney, William,	"	"	———; from wounds.
Messer, Charles E.,	"	"	March 23, 1862.
O'Brien, Edward,	"	"	February 6, 1863; from wounds.
Powers, Matthew E.,	"	"	April 19, 1862.
Reddy, Andrew,	"	"	October 12, 1862; from wounds.
Ryder, Thomas,	"	"	———

Transferred.

Nathan Carns, 1st Sergeant, to Non-Commission Staff; promoted Sergeant Major, April 1, 1863.

Edward C. Scott, Sergeant, to 32d Mass. Vols, June 9, 1864.

Edward Hegan, " to Vet. Res. Corps.

Company D — *continued.*

James Shea,	Sergeant,	to 32d Mass. Vols.,	June 9, 1864.
John O'Brien,	Corporal,	"	" "
John L. Benden,	Musician,	"	" "
Baker, Charles,	Private,	"	" "
Buchan, William,	"	"	" "
Bell, Richard,	"	to Company F,	April 5, 1863.
Carr, James, 2d,	"	to 32d Mass. Vols.,	June 9, 1864.
Cassidy, Peter,	"	to Vet. Res. Corps.	
Curran, John,	"	to 32d Mass. Vols.,	June 9, 1864.
Cleveland, William,	"	"	" "
Doherty, Michael,	"	"	" "
Dowd, Peter,	"	"	" "
Durant, Charles,	"	"	" "
Dunn, John,	"	to Vet. Res. Corps,	Dec. 18, 1863.
Fuller, Ezekiel,	"	"	
Fairbanks, Charles L.,	"	to 32d Mass. Vols.,	June 9, 1864.
Gill, Joseph,	"	to Vet. Res. Corps,	Oct. 30, 1863.
Guiney, William,	"	to 32d Mass. Vols.,	June 9, 1864.
Haggerty, John,	"	"	" "
Hanson, John,	"	to the Navy,	April 21, 1864.
Hill, Thomas H.,	"	to 32d Mass. Vols.,	June 9, 1864.
Hughes, Edward,	"	to Vet. Res. Corps.	
Jackson, Andrew,	"	to 32d Mass. Vols.,	June 9, 1864.
Kenney, Dennis,	"	"	" "
Kevlin, Thomas,	"	"	" "
Kevlin, Richard,	"	"	" "
Killan, Thomas,	"	"	" "
Leppart, John,	"	"	" "
Lancy, John,	"	to the Navy,	April 21, 1864.
Lee, Walter,	"	to 32d Mass. Vols.,	June 9, 1864.
McGowan, Thomas,	"	"	" "
McDonough, James,	"	to Company I.	
McCormack, Thomas,	"	to 32d Mass. Vols.,	June 9, 1864.
O'Donnell, Owen,	"	"	" "
Walsh, Patrick,	"	"	" "
Walsh, John,	"	"	" "

Company D — *continued.*

Deceased.

Patrick Collins, First Sergeant, killed at the battle of Gaines' Mills Va., June 27, 1862.
John D. Doherty, Sergeant, killed at the battle of Shady Grove Church, Va., May 30, 1864.
James I. Haley, Corporal, killed at the battle of the Wilderness, Va., May 5, 1864.
James McCam, Corporal, killed at the battle of the Wilderness, Va., May 5, 1864.
John Reed, Corporal, died of wounds, May 18, 1864.
Cartwright, John, Private, died of wounds, June 27, 1862.
Conway, Michael, Private, killed at the battle of Malvern Hill, Va., July 1, 1862.
Flynn, John, Private, killed at the battle of Gaines' Mills, June 27, 1862.
McConologue, Neal, Private, killed at the battle of Gaines' Mills, June 27, 1862.
McKenna, Francis, Private, killed at the battle of Gaines' Mills, Va., June 27, 1862.
McFeeley, William, Private, killed at the battle of Gaines' Mills, Va., June 27, 1862.
McGrade, Terrence, Private, died of wounds, June 27, 1862.
McLaughlin, John, Private, died of wounds, July 1, 1862.
O'Hara, John, Private, killed at the battle of Laurel Hill, Va., May 8, 1864.
Provost, Mitchell, Private, killed at the battle of Malvern Hill, Va., July 1, 1862.
Regan, Peter, Private, died of disease, December 19, 1862.
Russell, Michael, Private, died of disease, December 9, 1862.
Tate, William I., Private, died from wounds, July 1, 1862.
Weimar, Conrad, Private, killed by accident on cars, June 13, 1864,
Walsh, James, Private, killed at the battle of the Wilderness, Va., May 5, 1864.
White, Stephen, Private, died of disease, January 14, 1863.

(Deserters dropped.)

Company E.

James McMullen, First Sergeant, mustered out June 21, 1864.
James Blakeney,	"	"	"	"
Martin Jenkins,	"	"	"	"
Anthony Mahler,	"	"	"	"
Charles Farmer,	"	"	"	"
John Hallman,	Corporal,	"	"	"
Daniel Ivers,	"	"	"	"
John Breen,	"	"	"	"
John Danehey,	"	"	"	"
Samuel Smith,	"	"	"	"
John Keating,	"	"	"	"
Thomas Carter,	"	"	"	"
Buckley, Daniel,	Private,	"	"	"
Bannon, John,	"	"	"	"
Barry, Patrick,	"	"	"	"
Breen, John,	"	"	"	"
Bush, Richard,	"	"	"	"
Coffey, Jeremiah,	"	"	"	"
Connors, Terence,	"	"	"	"
Clure, Michael,	"	"	"	"
Connoy, Michael,	"	"	"	"
Darney, Daniel,	"	"	"	"
Daveron, Michael,	"	"	"	"
Dorrington, Hugh,	"	"	"	"
Doherty, Patrick,	"	"	"	"
Doherty, George F.,	"	"	"	"
Deidy, Thomas,	"	"	"	"
Grimes, Michael,	"	"	"	"
Henon, Patrick,	"	"	"	"
Hannally, David,	"	"	"	"
Kelley, Francis,	"	"	"	"
Mullain, Patrick,	"	"	"	"
Morrison, John,	"	"	"	"
Malcolm, James,	"	"	"	"
McLaughlin, Michael,	"	"	"	"
Norton, Michael,	"	"	"	"

Company E — *continued.*

O'Callaghan, Eugene,	Private,	mustered out, June 21, 1864
Palmer, William E.,	"	" " " "
Punch, John,	"	" " " "
Quigley, Martin,	"	" " " "
Regan, Timothy,	"	" " " "
Sullivan, Dennis,	"	" " " "
Walsh, Patrick,	"	" " " "

Discharged.

Philip Redmond, First Sergeant, to accept commission, March 22, 1863. (See Officers' Roster.)

Daniel Ford, Sergeant, for disability from wounds, Feb. 27, 1863.

Thomas Ivers, Sergeant, by order of War Department, September 1, 1862.

Gaffney, Patrick,	Corporal, for disability,	January	11, 1863.
Sullivan, Thomas,	Corporal, "	Nov.	17, 1862.
Boyle, Patrick,	Private, "	October	4, 1862.
Barker, James,	" "	"	25, 1861.
Bloomis, William,	" "	September	1, 1863.

Blood, William J., Private, to accept commission, Sept. 26, 1862. (See Officers' Roster.)

Cronan, Jeremiah,	Private, for disability,	October	25, 1862.
Carroll, John,	" "	Dec.	27, 1862.
Cassidy, John,	" "	February	5, 1863.
Dolan, Patrick,	" "	Dec.	23, 1861
Deerin, John,	" "	March	5, 1863.
Durkin, Patrick,	" "	Dec.	25, 4862.

Fogerty, William, Private, by order War Dep't, September 1, 1862.

Frye, William F.,	Private, for disability,	Nov.	19, "
Gallagher, John,	Private, "	March	18, "
Hennessy, Thomas,	" "	August	30, 1862.
Hayes, Charles,	" "	January	31, 1863.
Harrigan, Timothy,	" "	Nov.	17, 1862.
Kelley, Michael,	" "	October	13, 1862.
Lynch, Henry,	" "	August	19, 1861.
McKenna, Patrick,	" "	March	7, 1862.

Mulroy, John, Private, by order of War Dep't, Sept. 1, 1862.

Company E — continued.

McCance, Daniel,	Private, by order of Gen. Morris,		Nov.	20, 1862.
McGooish, Thomas,	Private,	for disability,	Nov.	22, 1862.
Mann, John A.,	"	"	February	14, 1863.
Mullen, Robert,	"	"	March	19, 1863.
Meagher, Patrick,	"	"	March	25, 1863.
Nary, Patrick,	"	"	Sept.	29, 1862.
Quinlan, Thomas,	Private for disability,		Dec.	18, 1862.

Regan, Matthew, Private, by order of General Wadsworth, August 7, 1862.

Rooney, Thomas,	Private, for disability,		Dec.	13, 1862.
Ryal, William,	"	"	Jan.	21, 1864.
Sullivan, John,	"	"	Dec.	20, 1862.
Sullivan, Daniel J.,	"	"	February	26, 1863.
Spellman, John,	"	"	June	17, 1863.
Veniker, William,	"	"	Dec.	11, 1862.
Walsh, James,	"	"	August	3, 1863.
Walsh, Edward,	"	"	February	4, 1863.

White, Thomas L., Private, by order of War Department, February 7, 1862.

Transferred.

Daniel G. Macnamara, First Sergeant, to Non-Commission Staff, March 10, 1862.

James W. Macnamara, Sergeant, to Company I, July 1, 1861.

Brady, Patrick,	Private,	to 32d Mass. Vols.,	June	9, 1864.
Butcher, James,	"	"	"	"
Creeley, William,	"	"	"	"
Carr, Joseph,	"	"	"	"
Carlton, Patrick,	"	"	"	"
Dwyer, Patrick,	"	to Vet. Reserve Corps,	May	5, 1864.
Gordon, George,	Corporal,	to 32d Mass. Vols.,	June	9, 1864.
Hunt, Peter,	Private,	to Vet. Res. Corps,	July	1, 1863.
Hewitt, Francis,	"	to 32d Mass. Vols.,	June	9, 1864.
Kennedy, Dennis,	"	"	"	"
Monaghan, Bernard,	"	to Vet. Res. Corps,	Aug.	1, 1863.
McDavitt, John,	"	"	April	9, 1864.
Mullen, Robert,	"	to 32d Mass. Vols.,	June	9, 1864.
O'Connor, Patrick,	"	to Vet. Res. Corps.,	Sept.	15, 1863.

Company E — continued.

O'Neill, John,	Private,	to 32d Mass. Vols.	June 9, 1864.
O'Connor, Daniel,	"	"	"
Powers, Benjamin,	"	to Company A,	Aug. 30, 1863.
Robson, James,	"	to 32d Mass., Vols.,	June 9, 1864.
Story, Nathaniel E.,	"	"	"
Smyth, James,	"	"	"
Scanlon, Thomas,	"	to the Navy,	February, 1862.
Webber, Louis,	"	to Vet. Res. Corps.	Sept. 1, 1863.

Deceased.

Ash, Frank, Private, killed at the battle of Spottsylvania, May 12, 1864.

Butler, Walter, Private, died of disease, June 15, 1862.

Boylan, Patrick, Private, died of wounds, July 13, 1862.

Condon, Richard, Corporal, killed at the Battle of the Wilderness, Va., May 5, 1864.

Condon, James, Private, killed at the Battle of Gaines' Mills, Va., June 27, 1862.

Collins, Edward, Private, died of wounds, January 11, 1861.

Cahill, Timothy, Private, killed at the Battle of Gaines' Mills, Va., June 27, 1862.

Enright, Michael, Private, died of disease, January, 11, 1863.

Fitzgerald, Michael, Private, killed at the Battle of Gaines' Mills, Va., June 27, 1862.

Garland, Owen, Private, drowned in Potomac River, June 27, 1861.

Gallagher, Owen, Private, killed at the Battle of Malvern Hill, Va., July 1, 1862.

Horan, Michael, Private, died of wounds, June 29, 1862.

Lambert, Joseph, Private, killed at the Battle of Gaines' Mills, Va., June 27, 1862.

Lynch, Martin, Private, died of wounds, December 31, 1863.

Murphy, Thomas, Private, killed at the Battle of the Wilderness, Va., May 4, 1864.

Maloney, James, Private, killed at the Battle of the Wilderness Va., May 5, 1864.

Moore, Richard, Private, killed at the Battle of Spottsylvania, Va., May 12, 1864.

Company E — continued.

Marvin, Thomas, Private, killed at the Battle of Gaines' Mills, Va. June, 27, 1862.
Newell, John B., Sergeant, killed at the Battle of Spottsylvania, Va. May 12, 1864.
Nole, James P., Private, killed at the Battle of Spottsylvania, Va. May 12, 1864.
Rourke, Dennis, Private, died of wounds, September 6, 1862.
Ross, Henry, Private, killed at the Battle of Laurel Hill, Va., May 8, 1862.
Smith, Charles D., Private, killed at the Battle of Laurel Hill, Va., May 8, 1862.
Sullivan, Michael, Private, died of wounds, June 29, 1862.
Smith, Joseph F., died of wounds, June 29, 1862.

(Deserters dropped.)

Company F.

Michael W. Boyle, First Sergeant, mustered out June 21, 1864.

John Lanigan,	Sergeant,	"	"	"
Thomas Fallon,	"	"	"	"
Edward Gugle,	"	"	"	"
Garrett Timmings,	"	"	"	"
Patrick Timmings,	Corporal,	"	"	"
Richard Carney,	"	"	"	"
James McLauglin,	"	"	"	"
Benjamin Hayes,	"	"	"	"
David Cashin,	"	"	"	"
John Ryan,	"	"	"	"
Patrick Tierney,	"	"	"	"
David Delaney,	Wagoner,	"	"	"
Barclay, Frank,	Private,	"	"	"
Connelly, James,	"	"	"	"
Cashin, Robert,	"	"	"	"
Creedin, Cornelius,	"	"	"	"
Cunningham, Lawrence,	"	"	"	"
Cain, Patrick,	"	"	"	"
Dempsey, James,	"	"	"	"

COMPANY F — *continued.*

Donavan, John,	Private,	mustered out, June 21, 1864.
Desmond, Dennis,	"	" " "
Dowdal, Charles,	"	" " "
Daley John,	"	" " "
Deemin, Michael,	"	" " "
Dennismore, William,	"	" " "
Daley, John, 2d,	"	" " "
Duggan, William,	"	" " "
Day, Ebenezer F.,	"	" " "
Flaherty, Thomas,	"	" " "
Gunning, John,	"	" " "
Gorham, William,	"	" " "
Hennessey, John,	"	" " "
Jordan, William,	"	" " "
Jenkins, James H.,	"	" " "
Kelley, Simon P.,	"	" " "
Kelley, John, 1st,	"	" " "
Kelley, John, 2d,	"	" " "
Keating, Michael,	"	" " "
Leslie, James,	"	" " "
McCarthy, Patrick,	"	" " "
McMahone, James,	"	" " "
Monaghan, Humphrey,	"	" " "
McFarland, James,	"	" " "
O'Keefe, Patrick,	"	" " "
O'Keefe, John,	"	" " "
O'Brien, Edward,	"	" " "
O'Roarke, John,	"	" " "
O'Shea, Timothy,	"	" " "
Sweeney, Daniel,	"	" " "
Scully, John,	"	" " "
Shea, Daniel,	"	" " "
Shortil, James,	"	" " "
Traines, Edward,	"	" " "
Walsh, Patrick,	"	" " "

Company F — *continued.*

Discharged.

Michael Phalen, First Sergeant, to accept commission, September 7, 1861. (See Officers' Roster.)

John Doherty, Sergeant, to accept commission, February 10, 1862. (See Officers' Roster.)

Martin O'Brien, First Sergeant, to accept commission, September 26, 1862. (See Officers' Roster.)

Burke, Uelic,   Private, for disability.
Burke, Charles,   "   "
Broderick, Dennis,   "   "
Bell, Richard,   "   "
Cogen, John,   "   "
Cullerton, Michael,   "   "
Callahan, Patrick,   "   "
Connor, James,   "   "
Cusic, Patrick,   "   "
Clines, John,   "   "
Cary, John,   "   "
Corcoran, Daniel,   "   "
Darah, Thomas,   "   "
Dolan, Patrick,   "   "
Doyle, James,   "   "
Driscol, John D.,   "   "
Hurley, William,   "   "
Hynes, John,   "   "
Kelley, Michael,   "   "
Kelley, James,   "   "
Kennedy, Martin,   "   "
Kelley, Charles D.,   "   "
Leary, Timothy,   "   "
Lynch, James, 1st,   "   "
Lynch, William,   "   "
Lynch, James, 2d,   "   "
McCarthy, Patrick,   "   "
McCarthy, Daniel,   "   "
Martin, James,   "   "
McGrath, John,   "   "

Company F — continued.

Martin, John,	Private for disability.		
Neal, Edward,	"	"	June 17, 1863.
O'Connor, James,	"	"	
O'Brien, John, 1st,	"	"	
O'Brien, John, 2d,	"	"	
O'Hara, Patrick,	"	"	June 18, 1862.
O'Brien, Thomas,	"	"	
Pender, John,	"	"	
Regan, Dennis,	"	"	
Ryan, Cornelius,	"	"	
Stephen, Joseph,	"	"	
Sweeney, Morgan,	"	"	
Smith, George B.,	"	"	
Twohey, John,	"	"	

Transferred.

Joseph Murphy, 1st Sergeant,	to Non-Com. Staff, Sept. 26, 1862.	
Joseph Monaghan, Sergeant,	" " "	
Boyd, Neil, Private,	to 32d Mass. Vols., June 9, 1864.	
Connor, William, "	" " "	
Connor, Thomas, "	to Vet. Res. Corps.	
Cullivane, Patrick, "	to 32d Mass. Vols., June 9, 1864.	
Dannings, Benjamin, "	to the Navy.	
Enei, William, "	to 32d Mass. Vols., June 9, 1864.	
Fitzpatrick, John, "	" " "	
Gordon, Samuel, "	" " "	
Lane, Martin, "	" " "	
Legere, Phillip, "	" " "	
Mahoney, Daniel D., "	to the Navy.	
Mattox, Harvey, "	to 32d Mass. Vols., June 9, 1864.	
Philman, Bernard, "	to Company B.	
Page, Benjamin, "	to 32d Mass. Vols., June 9, 1864.	
Redmond, William D., "	to the Navy.	
Shackleton, Joseph, "	to 32d Mass. Vols., June 9, 1864.	
Sweeney, Patrick, "	to the Navy.	

Roster of Enlisted Men.

Company F — *continued.*

Deceased.

James Connors, Private, died of disease.
William Regan, Private,   "   "
Patrick Shea, Private, died from wounds.
Thomas S. Sherlock, Private, died of disease.
John Tracey, Private, died of disease.
Robert Farrell, killed at the Battle of Gaines' Mills, Va., June 27, 1862.
John F. Tierney, Private, killed at the Battle of Gaines' Mills, Va., June 27, 1862.
John Granby, Private, killed at Battle of Malvern Hill, Va., June 27, 1862.
Morris Hurleighby, Private, killed at the Battle of Fredericksburg, Va., December 13, 1863.
Peter McNamara, Private, killed at the Battle of Gaines' Mills, Va., June 27, 1862.
John Morrissey, Private, killed at the Battle of Fredericksburg, Va., December 13, 1863.
Patrick Meagher, Private, killed at the Battle of Gaines' Mills, Va., June 27, 1862.
James Powers, Private, killed at the Battle of Shady Grove, 1864.
James Regan, Private, killed at the Battle of Gaines' Mills, Va., June 26, 1862.

(Deserters dropped.)

Company G.

Michael Murphy,	1st Sergeant, mustered out, June 21, 1864.		
Michael Clark,	Sergeant,	"	"
Francis Carey,	"	"	"
William H. Armstrong,	"	"	"
Thomas Hackett,	Corporal,	"	"
Timothy Quinn,	"	"	"
Thomas Brigham,	"	"	"
Maurice Sullivan,	"	"	"
Richard F. Murphy,	"	"	"

COMPANY G — *continued.*

Thomas Philbin	Musician,	mustered out,	June 21, 1864.	
Allen, Michael,	Private,	"	"	
Barry, Thomas,	"	"	"	
Creamer, Lawrence,	"	"	"	
Collins, James,	"	"	"	
Cowhey, Edward,	"	"	"	
Clark, Peter,	"	"	"	
Conboy, Thomas,	"	"	"	
Clancy, Thomas,	"	"	"	
Cunningham, William,	"	"	"	
Deneen, Thomas,	"	"	"	
Doherty, Patrick,	"	"	"	
Driscoll, John,	"	"	"	
Donavan, John,	"	"	"	
Davis, Willliam,	"	"	"	
Dolan John,	"	"	"	
Donavan, John E.,	"	"	"	
Gerrity, Patrick,	"	"	"	
Haggerty, Michael,	"	"	"	
Lanigan, James,	"	"	"	
Linnehon, Dennis,	"	"	"	
Lowe, John,	"	"	"	
Lovell, George,	"	"	"	
McGuire, Thomas,	"	"	"	
McHugh, Patrick,	"	"	"	
McHugh, Cornelius,	"	"	"	
McCann, Michael,	"	"	"	
McQueeny, Peter,	"	"	"	
Murnane, William,	"	"	"	
Murphy, John,	"	"	"	
Oscar, Eli,	"	"	"	
O'Brien, Patrick,	"	"	"	
Rice, Thomas,	"	"	"	
Riley, Maurice,	"	"	"	
Sweeny, Edward,	"	"	"	
Smith, Bernard,	"	"	"	
Stone, Lewis,	"	"	"	

Roster of Enlisted Men.

Company G — *continued*.

Tobin, Michael,	Private,	mustered out, June 21, 1864.
Walsh, Walter,	"	" "

Discharged.

Edward Finnottie, First Sergeant, to accept commission, September 11, 1861. (See Officers' Roster.)

John Allen,	Corporal,	for disability,	October 18, 1862.
Burke, Patrick,	Private,	"	December 18, 1862.
Berrystren, Charles,	"	"	" "
Cotter, Michael,	"	"	October 23, 1861.
Creed, John,	"	"	March 8, 1862.
Cotter, Cornelius,	"	"	November 14, 1862.
Callahan, Dennis,	"	"	January 29, 1863.
Curran, Charles,	"	"	December 19, 1863.
Clements, Francis,	"	"	February 19, 1862.
Coughlin, Michael,	"	"	August "
Carey, James,	"	"	" "
Dooley, Thomas,	"	"	" 22, 1862.
Donovan, John,	"	"	March 8, "
Dempsey, Timothy,	"	"	August 3, "
Duggan, Patrick,	"	"	December 13, "
Duggan, Matthew,	"	"	February 5, "
Fahey, Martin,	"	"	December 13, "
Farley, Michael,	"	"	January 2, "
Fleming, John,	"	"	March 30, "
Feeley, John,	"	"	May 5, 1863.
Goodwin, James H.,	"	"	July 1, 1862.
Hayes, William,	"	"	August 3, "
Higgins, Timothy,	"	"	October 31, "
Kane, Henry,	"	"	August 25, 1861.
Kelley, Lawrence,	"	"	" 8, 1862.
Kenny, Bryan,	"	"	" 8, "
Keleher, William,	"	"	" 8, 1863.
Lovett, Charles,	"	"	October 25, 1861.
Mahoney, William,	"	"	February 29, 1864.
Mahoney, James,	"	"	January 21, 1862.
Murray, Patrick,	"	"	August 8, "

Company G — *continued.*

McDermott, Patrick,	Private, for disability,	August	22, 1861.
McLaughlin, James,	" "	February	16, 1863.
McCann, John,	" "	March	24, "
McEnery, John,	" "	"	30, "
Nervins, Edward,	" "	February	9, "
O'Brien, Richard,	" "	October	28, 1861.
O'Shaughnessy, Michael,	" "	"	13, 1862.
Prushio, Joseph,	Corporal, "	May	5, 1863.
Purbeck, John H.,	Private, "	August	"
Strachan, William,	" "		
Stewart, William,	" "	"	22, 1862.
Smith, John,	" "	November	25, "
Sullivan, Daniel,	" "	February	19, 1863.
Sullivan, Jeremiah,	" "	October	17, "
Walsh, Martin,	" "	April	22, "

Transferred.

Clifford, John,	Private, to 32d Mass. Vols., June	9, 1864.
Cassidy, Lawrence,	" " " "
Cleary, James,	" " " "
Dailey, Felix,	" " " "
Gammon, Lorenzo,	" " " "
Howard, William,	" to Vet. Res. Corps, Nov. 11, 1863.
Lyden, Martin,	" to 32d Mass. Vols., June 9, 1864.
Lavery, William,	" " " "
McEnery, William,	" " " "
Riordan, Michael,	" " " "
Smith, Thomas,	" " " "

Deceased.

Ahearn, Michael, Private, killed accidentally, September 12, 1862.

Buckley, John, Corporal, died of wounds, May 12, 1864.

Bumpus, Jedediah, Private, killed at the Battle of the Wilderness, Va., May 5, 1864.

Burns, Eugene, Private, died of disease, September 8, 1862.

Clark, Patrick, Private, killed at the Battle of Gaines' Mills, Va., June 27, 1862.

Company G — *continued.*

Cutter, Augustus, 1st, Private, died of disease, May 4, 1864.
Connor, John, First Sergeant, killed at the Battle of the Wilderness, Va., May 7, 1864.
Daly, Robert, First Sergeant, killed at the Battle of Malvern Hill, Va., July 1, 1862.
Duffy, Charles T., Private, died of disease, August 26, 1863.
Finnerty, Bartholomew, Private, killed at the Battle of Gaines' Mills, Va., June 27, 1862.
Furphy, Cornelius, Private, killed at the Battle of Malvern Hill, Va., July 1, 1862.
Fitzgerald, John, Private, died of disease, March 2, 1862.
Green, George L., Private, died of wounds, May 12, 1862.
Hughes, Peter, Private, killed at the Battle of the Wilderness, Va., May 5, 1864.
Haggerty, John, Private, died of wounds, June 27, 1862.
Keleher, Cornelius, Private, died of disease, September 27, 1862.
Keating, William, Private, died of disease, September 17, 1862.
Long, Cornelius, Private, killed at the Battle of Gaines' Mills, Va., June 27, 1862.
Maloy, Patrick, Private, killed at the Battle of the Wilderness, Va., May 5, 1864.
Mahoney, John, Private, killed at the Battle of Malvern Hill, Va., July 1, 1862.
Quinn, Charles, Private, killed at the Battle of Gaines' Mills, Va., June 27, 1862.
Regan, Daniel I., Sergeant, killed at the Battle of Hanover Court House, May 27, 1862.
Sheehan, James, Corporal, died of disease, January 3, 1863.
Stiles, Lewis H., Private, killed accidentally, February 29, 1864.
Winters, Lawrence, Private, died of disease, September 6, 1862.
Scollard, Patrick, Private, killed at the Battle of Gaines' Mills, Va., June 27, 1864.

Missing in Action.

Burns, Michael, Corporal, at the Battle of Laurel Hill, Va., May 12, 1864.
Feely, Richard, Sergeant, at the Battle of Laurel Hill, Va., May 12, 1864.

COMPANY G — *continued.*

Flynn, David, Private, at the Battle of Laurel Hill, Va., May 12, 1864.
Foley, John, Private, at the Battle of Laurel Hill, Va., May 12, 1864.
Walker, Silas, Private, at the Battle of Laurel Hill, Va., May 12, 1864.

(Deserters dropped.)

Company H.

Patrick Doherty, First Sergeant, mustered out June 21, 1864.
John H. Donovan, Sergeant, " " "
Malachi Curley, " " " "
Andrew Pratt, " " " "
Patrick Blunt, " " " "
William Ford, Corporal, " " "
Patrick McGuillian, " " " "
David Slattery, " " " "
John W. Griffin, " " " "
John P. Donovan, " " " "
Patrick White, " " " "
Timothy, Desmond, " " " "
Daniel Sullivan, " " " "
Timothy Conaughton, Wagoner, " " "
Burke, Michael, Private, " " "
Burke, David, " " " "
Broderick, William, " " " "
Brady, Peter, " " " "
Burke, Michael D., " " " "
Burke, Samuel, " " " "
Connors, James, " " " "
Cronin, John, " " " "
Carey, William J., " mustered out, June 27, 1864.
Carr, John W., " " " "
Carr, John, " " " "
Conroy, John, " " " , "
Connors, William, " " " "

Company II — continued.

Doherty, Patrick,	Private,	mustered out,	June 27, 1864.	
Dillon, Jeremiah,	"	"	"	"
Driscoll, Michael,	"	"	"	"
Doherty, John,	"	"	"	"
Doherty, Patrick B.,	"	"	"	"
Finton, Thomas,	"	"	"	"
Fitzpatrick, Edward,	"	"	"	"
Griffin, John,	"	"	"	"
Hart, Henry,	"	"	"	"
Murray, John,	"	"	"	"
McCarthy, Patrick,	"	"	"	"
Murphy, Michael,	"	"	"	"
McLaughlin, Edward,	"	"	"	"
McNeil, James,	"	"	"	"
McCormack, James,	"	"	"	"
Regan, Joseph,	"	"	"	"
Shea, John,	"	"	"	"
Slattery, Thomas,	"	"	"	"
Tiernan, Marcus,	"	"	"	"

Discharged.

John McAveny,	Private, for disability,	October	29,	1861.
Merrick Cowells,	" "	"	"	"
Dennis O'Neil,	Sergeant, "	September 17,	1862.	
John Whalen,	Private, "	October	15,	"
Michael B. McMahon,	" "	March	1,	"

Daniel Callahan, Private, for disability, October 1, 1862; from wounds.

John F. Toomey, Private, for disability, October 25, 1862.

John Clifford, Private, for disability, October 27, 1862; from wounds.

Patrick Rowe, Private, for disability, October 30, 1862; from wounds.

Dennis Mooney, Private, for disability, October 30, 1862.

James Rowe, Private, for disability, October 22, 1862; from wounds.

Patrick Flynn, Private, for disability, September 26, 1862; from wounds.

COMPANY H — *continued.*

Daniel Sweeney, Private, for disability, September 22, 1862.
Maurice Cahill, Private, for disability, October 14, 1862.
John Cain, Private, for disability, November 8, 1862; from wounds.
John O'Grady, Private, for disability, December 31, 1862; from wounds.
Hugh Gilbridge, Private, for disability, January 13, 1863; from wounds.
James McGowan, Corporal, for disability, March 25, 1863; from wounds.
Francis Foley, Private, for disability, January 26, 1863.
James W. Tobin, Sergeant, for disability, April 6, 1863; from wounds.
John Sullivan, Private, for disability, January 31, 1863.
Michael Rogers, Private, for disability, October 30, 1862.
John O'Keefe, Private, for disability, November 2, 1862; from wounds.
Cornelius Fahey, Private, for disability, December 27, 1862.
Michael Coakley, Private, for disability, December 13, 1862; from wounds.

TRANSFERRED.

Michael A. Finnerty, Sergeant, to Non-Commission Staff, October 25, 1861.
Patrick E. Murphy, First Sergeant, to Non-Commission Staff, February 26, 1862.
William R. Burke, First Sergeant, to Non-Commission Staff, September 26, 1862.

Cornelius Carmody,	Private,	to Company A,	Aug.	9, 1861.
Patrick Daveron,	"	to Vet. Res. Corps,	Oct.	5, 1863.
John Donnelly,	"	"	Dec.	29, 1863.
Charles Willis,	"	"	"	" "
Bryan Connell,	"	"	July	27, "
James Corcoran,	"	"	Oct.	5, "
Patrick Smith,	"	"	Dec.	14, "
Hugh Weldon,	"	"	July	1, "
Thomas H. Adams,	"	to 32d Mass. Vols.,	June	9, 1864.
Michael J. Burke,	"	"	"	"

Roster of Enlisted Men.

Company H — *continued.*

John W. H. Bindon,	Private,	to 32d Mass. Vols., June	9, 1864.
James Donnelly,	"	"	"	"
Nehemiah S. Dodd,	"	"	"	"
John Foley,	"	"	"	"
John R. Goss,	"	"	"	"
John Holmes,	"	"	"	"
John Healey,	"	"	"	"
Edmund Lewis,	"	"	"	"
Patrick Ledon,	"	"	"	"
William McDonald,	"	"	"	"
John Melvin,	"	"	"	"
James J. Rix,	"	"	"	"
John B. Salkins,	"	"	"	"
Henry Young,	"	"	"	"
Francis Finnerty,	"	"	"	"
John J. Ford,	"	"	"	"
Patrick Fitzsimmons,	"	"	"	"
Owen McCarthy,	"	"	"	"
Michael Finnerty,	"	"	"	"
Francis Murray,	"	"	"	"
George Mitchell,	"	"	"	"
Thomas Mullen,	"	"	"	"
John Tobin,	"	"	"	"
Patrick Sweeney,	"	"	"	"
D. Sweeney,		"	to Bat. D, 5th U. S. Art., June 9, 1864.

Deceased.

Hugh Doherty, Private, drowned in Potomac River, September 26, 1861.

Michael Jordan, Private, died of disease, June 1, 1862.

Thomas Tynman, Private, died of disease, June 15, 1862.

Jeremiah Murphy, Private, killed at the Battle of Gaines' Mills, Va., June 27, 1862.

Samuel Day, Private, killed at the Battle of Gaines' Mills, Va., June 27, 1862.

Thomas Cummings, Private, killed at the Battle of Gaines' Mills, Va., June 27, 1862.

COMPANY H — *continued.*

Simon Carley, Private, killed at the Battle of Gaines' Mills, Va., June 27, 1862.
John O'Neil, Private, killed at the Battle of Gaines' Mills, Va., June 27, 1862.
William Adams, Private, killed at the Battle of Gaines' Mills, Va., June 27, 1862.
Thomas Hubon, Corporal, died of wounds, July 22, 1862.
James H. McGovern, Private, died of wounds, August 7, 1862.
Patrick, Holian, Private, killed at the Battle of Malvern Hill, Va., July 1, 1862.
Patrick Collins, Private, died of disease, October 21, 1863.
William McBrian, Private, killed at the Battle of Gaines' Mills, Va., June 27, 1862.
Jeremiah Ring, Private, killed at the Battle of Fredericksburg, Va., December 13, 1862.
William Peachy, Private, killed at the Battle of the Wilderness, Va., May 5, 1864.
James O'Connell, Private, killed at the Battle of the Wilderness, May 5, 1864.
John Mullen, Private, killed at the Battle of Laurel Hill, Va., May 8, 1864.
Thomas Nugent, Private, killed by accident, March 17, 1864.
James Dooley, Private, died of wounds, December 20, 1862.
William McLaughlin, Private, died of disease, January 2, 1863.
John F. Reilly, Private, died of disease, December 15, 1862.

(Deserters dropped.)

Company I.

Jeremiah Cronin,	1st Sergeant, mustered out June 21, 1864.			
Patrick J. Sullivan,	Sergeant,	"	"	"
Bernard McLaughlin,	"	"	"	"
Thomas Flynn,	"	"	"	"
David Brickley,	Corporal,	"	"	"
William Carroll,	"	"	"	"
Michael Dempsey,	"	"	"	"

Company I — *continued.*

Thomas Green,	Corporal,	mustered out, June 21, 1864.
Michael Roach,	"	" " " "
Patrick Herlihey,	"	" " " "
Boylan, Henry,	Private,	" " " "
Bourke, Patrick,	"	" " " "
Coughlin, James,	"	" " " "
Dolan, Thomas,	"	" " " "
Dacey, Cornelius,	"	" " " "
Fallan, Thomas,	"	" " " "
Fohey, Thomas,	"	" " " "
Flynn, Nicholas,	"	" " " "
Flynn, Edmond,	"	" " " "
Griffin, Patrick,	"	" " " "
Gallagher, John,	"	" " " "
Gallagher, Patrick,	"	" " " "
Hurley, Daniel,	"	" " " "
Leslie, James,	"	" " " "
Lehwellyn, Thomas,	"	" " " "
Mahoney, Dennis,	"	" " " "
Murphy, James,	"	" " " "
McCarthy, Charles,	"	" " " "
McCarran, Daniel,	"	" " " "
McAuliff, Patrick,	"	" " " "
McDermott, John,	"	" " " "
McGuire, Thomas,	"	" " " "
McKliget, James,	"	" " " "
Norton, Thomas,	"	" " " "
O'Brien, Daniel A.,	"	" " " "
Phalon, William,	"	" " " "
Quinn, John,	"	" " " "
Sherlock, Thomas,	"	" " " "
Spring, Patrick,	"	" " " "
Sullivan, Bernard,	"	" " " "
Slyman, John,	"	" " " "

Company I — *continued.*

Discharged.

James W. Macnamara, First Sergeant, to accept commission, October 20, 1862. (See Officers' Roster.)
Timothy Dacey, Sergeant, to accept commission, September 24, 1862. (See Officers' Roster.)
Lawrence Conlin, Sergeant, for disability, October 15, 1862 ; from wounds.
Andrew Doran, Corporal, for disability, February 12, 1863.
Joseph Barry, Corporal, for disability, September 1, 1862 ; from wounds.
Alcom, Thomas, Private, for disability, October 10, 1862.
Blake, George, Private, by order of the War Department, October 23, 1862.
Buckley, James, Private, for disability, November 28, 1862; from wounds.
Burns, William, Private, for disability, September 1, 1863.
Carney, Martin, Private, for disability, July 18, 1862.
Cullen, John, Private, for disability, November 19, 1862; from wounds.
Connell, William, Private, for disability, July 16, 1862.
Curtin, Daniel, Private, for disability, November 24, 1862.
Casey, Michael, Private, for disability, December 30, 1862.
Connors, John, Private, for disability, January 27, 1863.
Duffy, Michael, Private, for disability, from wounds.
Eddy, David, Private, for disability, April 15, 1863.
Garvey, Patrick, Private, for disability, October 28, 1862 ; from wounds.
Heeney, Richard, Private, for disability, March 25, 1863.
Jones, John, Private, for disability, April 13, 1864.
Keenan, John, Private, for disability, February 21, 1863.
Kirty, Michael H., Private, by order of the War Department, October 23, 1862.
Kelley, Timothy, Private, for disability, March 2, 1862.
Lane, Patrick, " " March 28, 1862.
Mundy, Bernard, " " September 21, 1861.
Moore, Patrick, " " January 2, 1862.
Morris, John, Private, disability from wounds, September 12, 1862.

Company I — continued.

McHugh, Hugh,   Private,   for disability,   November 24, 1862.
McCormack, John,   "   "   October   26, 1862.
McLaughlin, Hugh,   "   "   from wounds.
O'Neill, Patrick,   "   "   December 27, 1862.
Regan, Andrew, Private, for disability, from wounds, September 27, 1862.
Shields, Peter, Private, for disability, Aug. 21, 1862; from wounds.
Spillian, John, Private, for disability, Oct. 29, 1862; from wounds.
Sullivan, John P., Private, for disability, Oct. 28, 1862; from wounds.
Sullivan, Lawrence, Private,   "   ·   June   15, 1863.
Sweeny, Owen,   "   "   April   16, 1863.
Thompson, Peter,   " by order War Dpt., October 23, 1863.
Whalen, James,   " for disability,   March   25, 1863.
Walsh, John,   "   "   December 26, 1863.

Transferred.

Francis O'Dowd, Sergeant, to Non-Commission Staff, —— 1862.
Edward McDonald, Sergeant, to Company D, September 1, 1861.
Angel, John, Private, to Navy.
Beaman, Warren E., Private, to 32d Mass. Vols., June 9, 1864.
Butterfield, James,   "   "   "   "   "
Carney, Thomas,   "   "   "   "   "
Curran, Francis,   "   to Vet. Res. Corps., March 15, 1864.
Cartwright, John   "   to Company D,   Aug. 10, 1861.
Coy, Henry,   "   to 32d Mass. Vols., June 9, 1864.
Church, Spencer,   "   "   "   "   "
Donavan, Patrick,   "   to Company A,   Aug. 10, 1861.
Delacey, John,   "   to 32d Mass. Vols., June 9, 1864.
Flynn, John,   "   "   "   "   "
Hermann, Lewis A.,   "   to Navy.
Kelley, John,   "   to Company A,   Sept. 1, 1861.
Kohlbrand, Charles H., "   to 32d Mass. Vols., June 9, 1864.
Laren, Thomas,   "   "   "   "   "
McKeever, James,   "   "   "   "   "
McNeil, James,   "   "   "   "   "
O'Loughlin, Terrence, "   "   "   "   "
Perley, Stephen,   "   "   "   "   "
Palmer, John,   "   "   "   "   "

COMPANY I — *continued.*

Sheridan, Thomas,   Private, to 32d Mass. Vols., June 9, 1864.
Sling, Edward,   "   "   "   "
Tierney, Edward,   "   to Regt. Band,   July 1, 1862.
Thompson, Andrew,   "   to 32d Mass. Vols., June 9, 1864.
Way, George,   "   "   "   "

DECEASED.

Patrick Rabbitt, Sergeant, died of wounds, May 12, 1864.
Patrick Carroll, Corporal,   "   "   "
James Burns,   "   "   "   July 13, 1863.
Maurice Cotter, Corporal, killed at the Battle of Gaines' Mills, Va., June 27, 1862.
Bernard Hayes, Corporal, killed at the Battle of the Wilderness, Va., May 5, 1864.
Charles Kearney, Corporal, killed at the Battle of Gaines' Mills, Va., June 27, 1862.
James McDonough, Corporal, killed at the Battle of Gaines' Mills, Va., June 27, 1862.
Blake, Stephen, Private, killed at the Battle of the Wilderness, Va., May 5, 1864.
Curran, Patrick, Private, killed at the Battle of Gaines' Mills, Va., June 27, 1862.
Conlin, Michael P., Private, died of disease, April 16, 1863.
Fitzgibbons, John, Private, died of wounds, June 27, 1862.
Garrity, John, Private, killed at the Battle of Gaines' Mills, Va., June 27, 1862.
Gilles, William, Private, died of wounds, May 5, 1864.
Garrity, Michael, Private, died of wounds, June 17, 1864.
Hackett, Thomas, Private, killed at the Battle of the Wilderness, Va., May 5, 1864.
Hale, John H., Private, killed at the Battle of Laurel Hill, Va., May 8, 1864.
Kelley, John, Private, died of disease, November 16, 1861.
Kelley, Daniel, Private, died of disease, October, 23, 1862.
Manyan, Thomas, Private, killed at the Battle of Spottsylvania Court House, Va., May 12, 1864.
Mulcahey, David, Private, died of wounds, July 1, 1862.

Roster of Enlisted Men.

Company I — *continued.*

Matthews, Lawrence, Private, died of wounds, May 5, 1864.
Nagle, Patrick, Private, killed at the Battle of Gaines' Mills, Va., June 27, 1862.
Oakes, James, Private, died of disease.
Winn, William, Private, killed at the Battle of Gaines' Mills, Va., June 27, 1862.

Company K.

Maurice Condon, First Sergeant, mustered out, June 21, 1864.
William Linehan, Sergeant, " " "
William Mitchell, " " " "
Michael Connelly, " " " "
Edward Riordan, " " " "
John Donahue, Corporal, " " "
Patrick F. McGuire, " " " "
John J. Breen, " " " "
Patrick Cunningham, " " " "
Barry, Michael, Private, " " "
Barlow, Robert, " " " "
Burke, James, " " " "
Clifford, Thomas, " " " "
Collins, Charles O., " " " "
Crane, Denrick, " " " "
Cullen, James, " " " "
Cunningham, Roger, " " " "
Carroll, Thomas, " " " "
Dempsey, Patrick, " " " "
Deary, Lawrence, " " " "
Flynn, James, " " " "
Flynn, Patrick, " " " "
Gartland, John, " " " "
Garey, John, " " " "
Horan, Patrick, " " " "
Johnston, Edward, " " " "
Kenney, Patrick, " " " "
Lee, Robert, " " " "

Company K — continued.

Martin, Michael,	Private, mustered out, June 21, 1864.			
Mahoney, James,	"	"	"	"
Mooney, William,	"	"	"	"
McGuire, Michael,	"	"	"	"
McGowen, John,	"	"	"	"
Noonan, Thomas,	"	"	"	"
Spellman, Patrick,	"	"	"	"
Sullivan, Richard,	"	"	"	"
Toomey, Jeremiah,	"	"	"	"
Webb, James,	"	"	"	"
Welsh, Patrick,	"	"	"	"

Discharged.

Hugh McGunnigle, First Sergeant, to accept commission, October 21, 1862. (See Officers' Roster.)

Butler, James,	Private, for disability,	October 20, 1862.
Clark, Michael,	" by order,	October 15, 1862.
Coughlin, John,	" "	May 12, 1864.
Dooley, John,	" "	August 26, 1862.
Doherty, James,	" for disability,	November 8, 1862.
Gately, Martin,	" by order,	Decemb'r 22, 1863.
Goward, James,	" "	" 31, "
Harris, James,	" "	February 9, "
Haley, James D.,	" "	October 30, 1862.
Johnston, William E.,	" "	November 1, 1862.
Kelley, Martin,	" "	October 29, "
Landy, Patrick,	" "	July 5, "
Long, John,	" "	Nov. 11, "
Lanagan, Patrick,	" "	August 19, 1863.
Murray, Neal,	" "	Nov. 24, 1862.
Meloney, Charles,	" for disability,	March 9, 1863.
McGuire, David,	" "	Nov. 9, 1861.
Manning, Patrick,	" "	June 2, 1863.
O'Sullivan, James,	" "	January 3, 1862.
O'Sullivan, Thomas A.,	" by order,	October 30, "
Reilley, Thomas,	" for disability,	April 26, "
Reddy, Andrew,	" by order,	October 30, "

Company K — *continued.*

Roddy, Patrick,	Private, for disability,	March	22, 1863.
Sweeney, John,	" by order,	October	30, 1862.
Sheridan, Philip,	" for disability,	Dec.	1, "
Smith, David,	" by order,	May	15, 1863.
Trainer, Francis,	" "	Jan.	25, "
Walsh, Michael,	" for disability,	Dec.	1, 1862.
Wiley, Charles,	" by order.	October	12, "

Transferred.

Columbus, Anthony,	Private,	to 32d Mass. Vols., June	9, 1864.
Daney, Emanuel,	"	to U. S. Navy,	April 21, "
Doran, Christian,	"	to 32d Mass. Vols., June	9, "
Ebberhardt, Justin,	"	" "	"
Ford, Alexander,	"	to Veteran Reserve Corps.	
Galle, Hagar,	"	to 32d Mass. Vols., June.	9, 1864.
Hogan, James,	"	" "	"
Jackson, John,	"	to Veteran Reserve Corps.	
Kelley, Patrick,	"	to 32d Mass. Vols., June	9, 1864.
Rock, Christian,	"	" "	"
Lundergreen, John,	"	to Veteran Reserve Corps.	
Lingner, Adolphus,	"	to 32d Mass. Vols., June	9, 1864.
Nolde, William,	"	" "	"
Naphut, Mathias,	"	" "	"
Rosa, George,	"	" "	"
Schimedt, George,	"	" "	"
Sheror, John,	"	" "	"
Schaffer, William,	"	" "	"
Scannell, John,	"	" "	"
Steward, John,	"	" "	"
Sweeney, Patrick,	"	" "	"
Thede, William,	"	" "	"

Deceased.

Butler, John, Private, killed at the Battle of Gaines' Mills, Va., June 27, 1862.

Connell, Michael, Private, killed at the Battle of the Wilderness, Va., May 5, 1864.

COMPANY K — *continued.*

Cogger, John, Private, killed at the Battle of Laurel Hill, Va., May 8, 1864.

Dennison, Patrick, Private, killed at the Battle of Gaines' Mills, Va., June 27, 1862.

Dermody, Patrick, Private, killed at the Battle of Malvern Hill, Va., July 1, 1862.

Ford, Joseph, Private, killed at the Battle of Gettysburg, Pa., July 2, 1863.

Flynn, Joseph, Private, killed at the Battle of the Wilderness, Va., May 5, 1864.

Howard, Simon, Private, died of wounds, September 1, 1863.

Keleher, Patrick, Private, killed at the Battle of the Wilderness, Va., May 5, 1864.

Kerns, John, Private, killed at the Battle of Laurel Hill, Va., May 8, 1864.

McLaughlin, James, Private, died of wounds, November 12, 1863.

Murphy, Myles, Private, killed at the Battle of Laurel Hill, Va., May 8, 1864.

Murtagh, Thomas, Private, killed at the Battle of Laurel Hill, Va., May 8, 1864.

Riordan, Daniel, Private, killed at the Battle of Gaines' Mills, Va., June 27, 1862.

Riordan, Daniel, 2d, Private, killed at the Battle of Gaines' Mills, Va., June 27, 1862.

Scannell, John, Private, died of wounds, July 1, 1862.

Schimatt, William, Private, killed at the Battle of the Wilderness, Va., May 5, 1864.

Toomey, James, Private, died of wounds, January 1, 1863.

Tully, Bartlett, Private, killed at the Battle of Gaines' Mills, Va., June, 27, 1862.

O'Hare, Hugh, Private, killed at the Battle of Gaines' Mills, Va., June 27, 1862.

(Deserters dropped.)

www.ingramcontent.com/pod-product-compliance
Lightning Source LLC
Chambersburg PA
CBHW030810230426
43667CB00008B/1156